Complete Book of
Fast Break Basketball

Complete Book of
Fast Break Basketball

CLIFF ELLIS

PARKER PUBLISHING COMPANY, INC.   West Nyack, NY

© 1979 *by*

Parker Publishing Company, Inc.

West Nyack, N.Y.

*All rights reserved. No part of this book
may be reproduced in any form or by
any means, without permission in writing
from the publisher*

Library of Congress Cataloging in Publication Data

Ellis, Cliff.
   Complete book of fast break basketball.

   Includes index.
   1. Basketball coaching. 2. Basketball--Offense.
I. Title.
GV885.3.E37   796.32'3'077   78-11040
ISBN 0-13-156737-3

Also by the Author

Zone Press Variations for Winning Basketball

This book is dedicated to my wife Carolyn, our daughter Chryssa, and our son Clay, for their love and understanding.

HOW FAST BREAK BASKETBALL
WILL FIT YOUR NEEDS

The *Complete Book of Fast Break Basketball* contains the types of fast break situations used by my teams during ten successful years of coaching. Every dimension of fast break basketball has been covered in this book. The book gives the coach of any type team whether it be one that is little or tall, slow or fast, situations where he can take advantage of the opponent by fast breaking.

If you coach against zone defenses, you will be able to see how the zones work and how to destroy them with fast break basketball. You will see how pressing defenses work and why the fast break disrupts them. The book shows which fast break to use if your team has poor overall ball handlers and discusses the fast break for teams with good ball handling guards. The methods of teaching fast break situations such as filling lanes, teaching two on one principles, three on two situations, and four on three techniques are also covered in the book.

No matter what level you coach, whether it be elementary, junior high, high school, college, or pros, a fast break for you is in this book. A fast break for any type personnel you have is in this book.

The *Complete Book of Fast Break Basketball* shows how to fast break from every possible situation that occurs in basketball. Step-by-step diagrams and illustrations explain how to coach the fast break from various types of breaking situations such as missed field goals, made baskets, and procedures for fast breaking from the free-throw line. Here, too, are the necessary fundamentals of the fast break such as rebounding, outlet passes, dribbling, shooting, and ball handling. The *Complete Book of Fast Break Basketball* discusses the two guard break, the sideline break, and the controlled break which offers the coach different methods of fast breaking so it will fit his philosophy or style of play. This book describes ways to use the fast break against man to man and pressing defenses. How to fast break from various zone presses, a new dimension in fast break basketball, is covered thoroughly in Chapter 7. A complete conditioning program for pre-season, in season, and post season is also covered to help you prepare your players for fast break basketball. Various drills are diagrammed and illustrated to facilitate perfecting the fast break.

Fast break basketball produces champions. There are more champions who win with the fast break than not. Besides, it is the only way the pros play at the highest level of competition. Be a champion, utilize fast break basketball. You can find the break that will fit your needs in this book.

Cliff Ellis

Acknowledgments

To all the players that have played for me. They are the ones who have made my coaching career a happy and successful one. I wish them all success in life.

To all my relatives, especially my parents, for their love and understanding now and while I was growing up.

To my assistant coaches for their hard work and dedication.

To Don Fuoss, author and former football coach, for encouraging me to write.

To Dr. Frederick P. Whiddon, President of the University of South Alabama, and Dr. Mel Lucas, Athletic Director at the University of South Alabama, for their wholehearted support and interest in the basketball program.

To Sandra McFarland for typing of the manuscript.

CONTENTS

13

Complete Book of
Fast Break Basketball

1

SHAPING THE FAST BREAK

The most exciting part of basketball today is the fast break. The fast break creates much excitement for the fans and they are the ones who are the backbone of any program. The thrill of seeing players racing up and down the floor scoring baskets can transform the game into pandemonium. Just think how many times a packed gym goes crazy because of great fast break execution.

Besides fan excitement, one of the main reasons to use the fast break is to keep teams from changing defenses or throwing a variety of presses at the offense. A team's goal should be to get the ball down the floor so quickly that opposing teams cannot press or change defenses quickly.

Players love the fast break. Let's face it: today's players like the fast game. They want to move. It provides them with the opportunity to score quickly and more often. I remember being

behind 12 points in one game with 1½ minutes to play; fast breaking off our steal situations won the game.

Creating an advantage over the opponent is another reason to
fast break. Anytime you can get two on one, three on two, four on
three, or five on four situations against an opponent you are at an
advantage. Fast breaking creates these opportunities. Two on two
and three on three situations are more favorable scoring situations
than the five on five because there is much more area and less
congestion for the offensive player to maneuver in.

The fast break maintains conditioning. You cannot be successful with the fast break unless you are in good condition. I have
devoted a chapter to conditioning later in the book because I feel it
is an important key to a successful fast break. Still, by utilizing the
fast break in practice and in games a player maintains his conditioning sufficiently to execute other phases of the game, such as half
court offenses and pressing defenses.

A successful team is one that is aggressive and the fast break is
aggressive basketball. The team that utilizes the fast break is taking
the fight to his opponent and this is what a winner wants.

The psychological damage that the fast break does is also a
factor in using the break. So many times teams have been in see-
saw battles with opponents and all of a sudden, after the fast break
produces four or five quick buckets, "bang" the ball game has been
broken open. I have seen teams get completely blown out of the
gym in a matter of minutes because of the fast break.

Fast break basketball is pressure offense. It keeps the pressure on your opponent at all times. This type of basketball is fantas-
tic in complementing pressure defenses because it provides you
with pressure on the opponent the entire game. We are a team that
uses a variety of pressure defenses as I explained in my book *Zone
Press Variations for Winning Basketball*. The fast break complements our defense in that our fast break offense comes at them so
fast that it keeps pressure on their defense.

THE PLAYER-COACH ROLE FOR A SUCCESSFUL FAST BREAK

Possibly the most important role played by the coach is that of
motivator. Some players never need motivating, but most players

will need it at one time or another. A coach never wants to see any of his players giving only 50 percent effort. For you to have an effective fast breaking team, every member must give it his maximum effort or you will lose out in the end. Therefore, if you want a successful fast break and a successful team, you must motivate. The coach's personality, convictions, and goals are important to the development of the attitudes of his athletes and to the degree of success they will achieve. You must examine the qualities you think are important in developing a winner. These qualities will become a part of the team character.

A coach is an effective motivator in all aspects of play if he can inspire aggressiveness, hard work, organization, and team spirit to a high degree. A coach cannot be weak in any of these areas or motivation will fail. For example, a coach cannot emphasize hard work, yet cut his practices too short; nor can he stress organization and planning, but be himself a careless person.

A problem facing all coaches is motivating the athlete externally while, at the same time, providing him with information regarding his play. The coach can have the player do what he wants by both praising and punishing. The difference is that with praise the athlete will end up with a more positive attitude toward the coach, the competition, and himself.

Praise gives the athlete an idea of what is correct. Punishment does not. It does nothing toward building positive feelings. Punishment creates doubt and confusion in the player regarding his ability and the coach's ability to help him. To get angry at a player because he is not intelligent, because he does not understand, because he is confused, or because he is frightened usually has a negative effect on the athlete's performance. It only succeeds in relieving the coach's anger. It does not help the athlete. If a player is not picking up the information because he is not paying attention or because he is lazy, then he needs to be attacked on that basis. This is a legitimate reason for the coach's anger, because the athlete is not only breaking a rule, but also harming himself.

There will be a few players with whom the coach will not be able to work, no matter how hard he tries. Before the coach finally gives up on the player completely, he might try a direct confrontation. He can be extremely open with the person by telling him

exactly how he feels about him and by giving him an honest evalua-
tion of his performance. The coach can make it clear to the athlete
that his membership on the team is over unless he does certain
very specific things within very specific time periods. If this ap-
proach fails, the coach can feel perfectly secure that he has done his
best.

PERFECTING SHOOTING, DRIBBLING, AND BALL HANDLING TECHNIQUES FOR FAST BREAK BASKETBALL

What good is any fast break when you cannot shoot or handle
the ball properly? Certain shooting, dribbling, and ball handling
fundamentals help secure the fast break.

The biggest thing to stress in shooting to develop the fast
break is the bank shot off the glass. Most fast break situations score
quickly from the wing area *(Diagram 1–1)* while a player is on the
move from 12 to 15 feet out. Because of the fast movement and
quickness in getting off the shot, players need to increase their
margins of error which the bank shot provides. Players should not
use the bank shot when in front of the basket. In teaching the bank
shot coaches should start out by having the player shoot the bank
shot from 12 to 15 feet out at the wing area while not moving. He
should learn to shoot the ball into the square above the rim on the

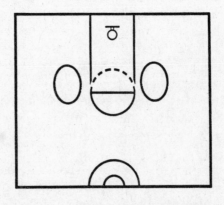

Diagram 1–1

glass so it will drop in with ease. This bank shot allows the ball to go in easier if it hits the rim.

After the player has learned the shot standing still, he learns to make the same shot coming off the move. *Diagram 1–2* shows the drill to help teach this shot off the move. 1 is the ball handler and dribbles the ball from the opposite free-throw line in back court and feeds the ball to 2 when he gets into the 12 to 15 feet wing area. 2 starts at the free-throw line extended in back court and goes full speed until he gets into the front court area near the hash mark where he must get himself under control. As he reaches the shooting area he receives the pass and tries to hit the bank shot off the move. As soon as he releases the ball, he comes down slightly forward to where he started to jump, as this momentum will help carry him to the goal for a follow-up shot in case of a miss.

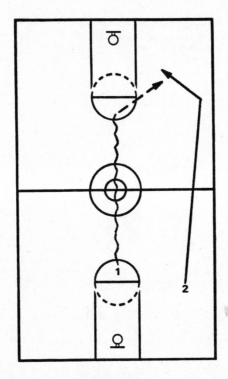

Diagram 1–2

There are various techniques in shooting that I feel are important whether teaching the bank shot or not. Some of the more important aspects of individual shooting that should be stressed thoroughly to all players include the following techniques:

1. The player must release the ball as he is reaching the height of his jump;
2. Push the shooting arm up rather than out and point the middle and index finger into the basket, rotating the hand forward and out;
3. Use the 5 c's of shooting: concentration, conformity of shot, confidence, courage to practice, and competitiveness;
4. As an individual, know what is a good percentage shot for himself;
5. Be a shooter and not a gunner;
6. Hurry getting ready, but do not hurry to shoot.

Dribbling drills should be used year round. Players can utilize these drills from day one of practice until the last day because poor dribbling kills the fast break. Players must be able to get the ball down the court to get the fast break.

The speed dribble is the most important dribble to the fast break. The ball handler who gets the outlet pass for a fast break must be able to get from the top of the key in back court to the top of the key in front court in 3 seconds with only 3 dribbles. The goal here is to get the ball down the floor in the least amount of time with as few dribbles as possible. The dribble to use to perfect this is shown in *Diagram 1–3*. 1 is the rebounder of a missed shot and makes an outlet pass to 2 at the top of the key in the back court. 2 starts the drill at the free-throw line extended and, as 1 gets the rebound, moves quickly to the top of the key where he will receive the pass and try to get to the top of the key in the front court in 3 seconds with only 3 dribbles.

Any defense today is going to try to stop the offensive player from dribbling the way he wants to; therefore, teach your players every possible dribbling situation that might occur in fast break situations. Every day at practice a team can use various dribbling drills to enable the ball handlers to deal with any type of dribbling situation they might face during the fast break. These drills are used full court with each player going down the floor using his right hand and returing using his left hand. A team can use three lines as shown in *Diagram 1-4* in developing its dribbling techniques. Every dribble that uses change of direction, change of pace, or change of hands is done at the free-throw line extended in back court, the ten second line, and the free-throw line extended in the front court. For example, a player that is executing a behind the back dribble will dribble behind his back at the free-throw line extended in back court, the ten second line, and the free-throw line extended in front court going down and coming back.

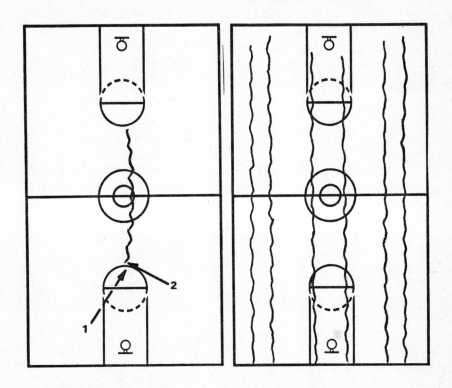

Diagram 1-3   Diagram 1-4

The following dribbling drills are the drills to use every day to help perfect the fast break. The Basic 7 dribbling drills are:

1. Right hand speed dribble
2. Left hand speed dribble
3. Behind the back dribble
4. Between the legs dribble
5. Reverse dribble
6. Stop and go dribble (Player must make a complete stop at the three intervals.)
7. Drop to one hand and make a complete circle (This is used in case a player falls down in a game situation and must maintain possession of the ball.)

Another important fundamental aspect of the fast break is adequate ball handling. This goes hand in hand with dribbling and passing, but teaching ball handling fundamentals does one particular thing I like, and that is it gives the player confidence with the basketball. The more things he can do with the basketball the more confident he is. A coach should want players to be as confident with the ball as they can be in game situations because this goes a long way toward winning.

The following ball handling drills are drills to use every day before practice to instill confidence in players when they have the ball.

1. Circle left leg 10 times as quickly as possible
2. Circle right leg 10 times as quickly as possible
5. Figure 8 between the legs 10 times as quickly as possible
4. Around the back 10 times as quickly as possible
5. Spin the ball on right fingertips for 10 seconds
6. Spin the ball on the left fingertips for 10 seconds

PASSING AND CATCHING FUNDAMENTALS TO DEVELOP YOUR FAST BREAK

Just as important as the fundamentals of shooting, dribbling, and ball handling are to the success of the fast break, so, too, are the fundamentals of passing and catching. Of course, the basic passes, such as the chest pass, bounce pass, and overhead pass, are important to any offensive phase of basketball. These are passes that a player develops in his younger years, but there are certain passes and passing techniques in addition to these that are vitally important to fast break basketball.

One of the most important passes in the fast break is the baseball pass, yet coaches sometimes overlook this pass and fail to teach it. Poor outlet passes break up a fast break attempt so often that you should stress this pass to your players, especially because it is one that they do not automatically practice throughout the year; teach them and make them do it in practice. In teaching this, have the player assume a baseball stance. Let us assume he is going to throw with his right hand. His left foot should be in front of his right with his left hand in front of the ball and his right hand behind the ball ready to throw. The ball should be held above the right shoulder at ear level. The important technique to stress here that is too often neglected involves the left hand. Too many people do not use this hand for support and it should be used for two primary reasons; accuracy and stopping the ball if a defensive man comes to intercept the outlet pass. If a player uses only his right hand to make a baseball pass without the left hand supporting it, he cannot stop his momentum when an interceptor is in the line of the pass and will usually fumble the ball. Also using the left hand for support for a right handed baseball pass makes the outlet passer throw an overhead pass like the fast ball in baseball. I have found that most players who throw with the right hand without using the left hand for support will not throw an overhand pass but will usually "break his wrist" like a pitcher who throws a curve in baseball with the basketball doing the same thing. When this type of curve ball is thrown, it makes the ball much more difficult to catch. Keeping these techniques in mind, have the passer step through and follow through just as a pitcher does.

There are also various passes and passing techniques to teach players so that they are a little more sophisticated than teams that use only basic passes.

One of these passes is the behind the back pass. The reason to teach this is to open up every type of passing opportunity. We teach this drill starting at the ten second line as shown in *Diagram*

1–5. 1 dribbles from the ten second line to the free-throw line where he executes a behind the back pass on the move to 2 who will receive the pass for a lay up. You can also stress the bounce pass from behind the back using the same drill technique.

Probably the most neglected fundamental in basketball is catching. Many players, especially post players, do not know how to catch the basketball. The biggest thing to stress in catching the basketball is looking the pass all the way into the hands. This assures complete concentration. Also of vital importance is to have the hands and fingertips relaxed and not stiff for catching accuracy.

To improve catching the basketball, use a bad pass drill, stressing the fundamentals of catching. In this drill, make bad passes to the receiver, who must concentrate on catching the ball wherever it is thrown.

You can teach your players various stunts to use in developing their catching. One of these involves catching the ball behind the back. The player stands with the ball in front of him in both hands. He throws the ball up in the air, approximately eight feet higher than his head, and catches the ball with both hands behind his back. The coach must teach the player that when the ball is in the air, he must position himself so that the face is under the ball and keep the head and eyes up. It is also important to keep the back straight. Just before the ball hits him in the face, he must step

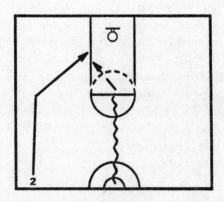

Diagram 1–5

forward with one foot and catch the ball behind the back in the hip area.

Another effective catching stunt includes catching the ball under the left leg with the left hand only. The player starts in a stride squat position with the left leg forward and the thighs parallel to the floor, holds the basketball between the legs with both hands, tosses the ball up approximately five feet in the air, reaches under the left leg with the left hand and catches the ball. This same drill can be done with the right hand and right leg.

REBOUNDING AND OUTLET TECHNIQUES

Since 75 percent of all fast break attempts occur after missed field goal attempts it is of the utmost importance that the fast breaking team get the rebound.

Some coaches today do not believe in blocking out. It is their feeling that with today's players having so much leaping ability that it is not necessary to block out. This is a questionable theory to adhere to. To get the majority of the rebounds a player must have the inside position on his opponent. Thus, blocking out for the rebound is a must. In teaching players to block out, set up an offensive man and defensive man six to eight feet from the bucket as shown in *Diagram 1–6*. A manager will shoot and miss the shot

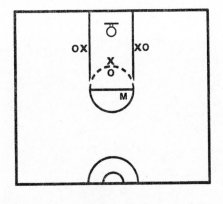

Diagram 1–6

with the defensive man supposedly getting the rebound. The defensive man, X, assumes a defensive position while the manager has the ball. When the ball is shot, the defensive man executes a quick jump. Keeping his feet as close to the floor as possible he makes an about face, as in the military, jumps to the goal with his head at an angle to see his opponent and the direction his opponent is going. Upon seeing the direction of the offensive man, he slides one step in his direction. By then if the opponent is going to the bucket for the ball he will feel the offensive man with his hands and buttocks thus keeping his opponent behind him and off balance. When the ball comes off the board he must get the ball by ripping it off the boards coming down with the ball in his hands, elbows spread, and feet well apart. When he learns to execute this technique he is ready to execute the outlet pass.

In making the outlet pass he will usually make the baseball pass. Both coach and player want this type of pass if they can get it but, of course, sometimes it is not there. If the immediate outlet is closed, the rebounder takes as long a stride as possible toward the side of the floor, putting the ball on the floor while looking for the man to make the outlet pass to. This is when the chest pass, bounce pass, and other basic passes come into play. The thing to remember is to execute the outlet pass quickly.

Just as important as the rebounder is the outlet man. His job is to do whatever it takes to get the ball even if it means coming back to the ball. The outlet man should never leave the rebounder stranded whether receiving the ball in the middle of the floor or up the sideline. Outlet men, receiving the ball in the middle of area, try to receive it in the top of the circle near the head of the key area. Sideline outlets should position as near the hash mark area as possible.

2

COACHING FAST BREAK
SITUATIONS

To be successful playing cards one must know how to determine odds and use them in his favor. The same is true in basketball. To be successful in fast break basketball a team must know
when the odds are in its favor. There are various opportunities such
as the two on one, three on one, three on two, four on three, and
five on four situations that the fast break will create. These are
situations that put the odds on scoring on the side of the fast break
team. The player must be taught to recognize when these odds are
in his favor because it is like this hypothetical half court pick up
game. A team with four men on offense will defeat a team with
three men on defense every time; therefore, fast break situations
like the four on three and three on two situations are going to be

triumphant. Coaches must stress that all the players in the game know the odds are in their favor.

The same awareness is necessary when the odds are not in favor of the fast break. If, for example, the three lanes are filled but there are four defensive men back on defense, it is a three on four situation and the defense will usually win out. So you must stress to your players that any time the fast break odds are not in their favor they should not pursue the fast break.

Determining the odds a team is facing is very important. It is a split second decision and if a coach does not stress to them to read situations a team is likely to come out on the short end in a game situation.

FILLING THE LANES

In the fast break, the court is divided into five lanes for the players to run in. These are the outside lanes on the left and right side of the court as shown in *Diagram 2–1;* the middle lane as shown in *Diagram 2–2;* and the two trailer lanes as shown in *Diagram 2–3.* The only time not to use a trailer lane is when a safety man is used in a fast break.

How the players fill these lanes is one of the more important factors in the fast break. If a player is filling an outside lane and does not receive the outlet pass from the rebounder, his job is to fill this lane as widely as possible and to be able to get from corner to corner in no more than four seconds. If he does not have the ball and the ball is in the middle lane and three lanes are filled, *Diagram 2–4,* and he has an opportunity for a layup or short jumper near the goal he should make a 45° angle cut to the basket from the free-throw line extended area. An important coaching point when a player is filling the right outside lane is that he must plant his right foot at the free-throw line extended area and push off it making his angle cut to the basket. It is also important that the player have his body under control in making the cut. A player in the left outside lane should use this same technique, planting his left foot and pushing off it. If a player receives an outlet pass in an outside lane and plans to fill this lane with the ball, he should use the speed dribble with as few dribbles as possible.

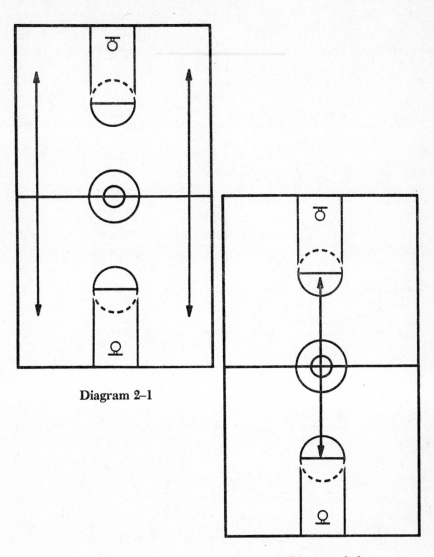

Diagram 2–1

Diagram 2–2

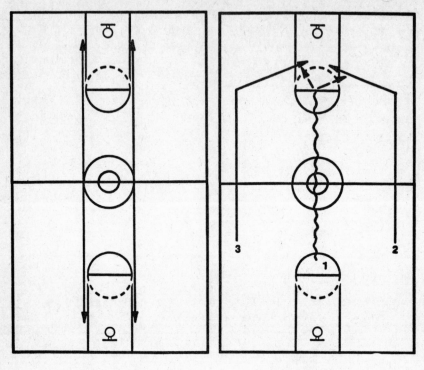

Diagram 2–3   Diagram 2–4

In most fast break attempts, the ball is usually in the middle lane. In this lane with the ball, the ball handler should be able to get from the bubble, shaded areas in *Diagram 2–5,* in the back court to the bubble in front court with three dribbles and in three seconds. This assures the team of a quick fast break attempt. Any player who fills the middle lane without the ball should get to the free-throw line in front court from the back court within three seconds after the ball has been rebounded.

The trailer lanes are usually filled by rebounders. They will be going after the rebound and as you can see in *Diagram 2–3* the trailer lanes go from the rebounding area in back court to the block areas in the front court. We want the players filling the trailer lanes to go for the rebound, make the outlet pass, and fill both the left and right trailer lanes. One of the trailer lanes will just about always be filled by the rebounder because he is usually the last to fill a lane. Once he makes the outlet pass he is to read which trailer lane one of the other rebounders filled. If his teammate fills the left trailer lane he will fill the right trailer lane and vice versa. In filling the trailer lanes, the players are told to sprint to the block area in the front court. They should be on the blocks ready for a pass to the post within four seconds after the outlet pass. The only exception is when they see that one of the men in the outside lane is going to get a layup from his cut which means he must stay clear of this post area as it may interfere with the layup shot.

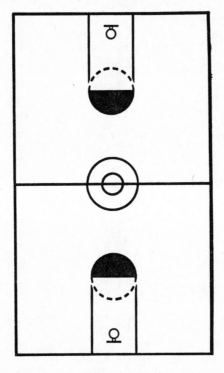

Diagram 2–5

TWO ON ONE AND THREE ON ONE PRINCIPLES

There are various times in a game when a two on one fast break situation will occur. This usually happens either on a steal or a long rebound by the defense. The two on one situation is illustrated in *Diagram 2–6*. 1, the ball handler, and 2 must keep wide angles which allows good spacing so that X, the defensive man, cannot guard both of them. It is the defensive man's job to try and make the offense take the longest and worst shot possible. Therefore, the ball handler, 1, must take the dribble right at X, the defensive man. If he does not commit he will get the layup. If he does commit he will have the pass to 2 for the easy shot as shown in *Diagram 2–7*.

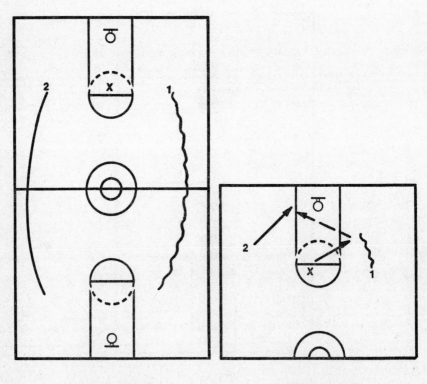

Diagram 2–6   Diagram 2–7

The three on one situation is very similar. Now the offense has three lanes filled and again they must make the defensive man commit as in *Diagram 2–8*. When he commits, the offense will have the easy pass to 2 or 3 in the outside lanes. If he does not commit, the ball handler can breeze past him for the layup without having to pass.

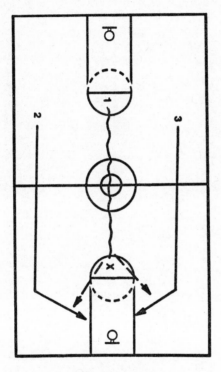

Diagram 2–8

THREE ON TWO SITUATIONS

The three on two fast break situation is probably the most common fast break situation. First let us look at the defensive assignment of the two defensive men, X1 and X2, in *Diagram 2–9*. It is X1's responsibility to stop the penetration of the ball as 1 steps inside the bubble as in *Diagram 2–10*. When this happens, 1 will usually pass to 2 or 3, 3 in this case in *Diagram 2–11*. When this pass is made, X2 defenses the ball and X1 slides back to protect the hole.

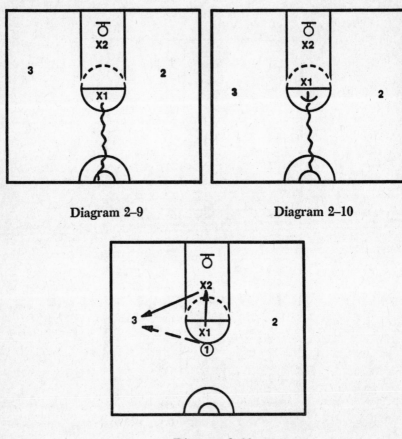

Diagram 2–9   Diagram 2–10

Diagram 2–11

If the three on two situation occurs and X1 does not commit and make the ball handler pick his dribble up, an easy shot will occur. The same is true as you can see if X2 does not stop the ball on the first pass. Most teams can stop penetration and the first pass, but this is where the three on two technique comes in. In *Diagram 2–12* as X2 stops the ball, 3, and X1 plugs the hole, 1 should step to the ball side of the floor for a return pass from 3. Now there is basically a two on one situation, 1 and 2 against X1. If X1 does not commit to 1 he has an easy jumper from the free-throw line. If X1 does commit, 1 should pass to 2 for an easy shot on his side of the floor.

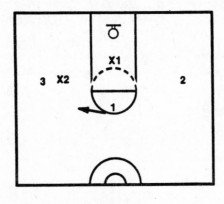

Diagram 2–12

FOUR ON THREE TECHNIQUES

Any time three men are defending the fast break, the usual procedure is for the first man back to plug the hole, the second man to stop the ball, and the third man to take the nearest man opposite the first pass. This is illustrated in *Diagram 2–13* with the middle, outside, and one of the trailer lanes being filled offensively. X1 and X2 are already back and X3 is in the process of retreating to stop the fast break. If, for example, X1 does his job, 1 will pass to 2 or 3—3 in this case. When the pass is made, *Diagram 2–14*, X2 will stop the ball, X1 will plug the hole and X3's job is to stop the most vulnerable man away from the pass, either 2 or 4. If the pass comes back to 1, *Diagram 2–15*, the usual procedure is for X1 to come back to the ball and X2 drop back to the hole. X3 now has two men in his area. This is where the four on three fast break should score if it does not score off the first pass. Of course, if a score does occur off

the first pass, the defense had a breakdown because the first pass of
the fast break in the front court can and should be stopped. Upon
the return pass from 3 to 1, *Diagram 2–15*, there is a two on one
situation on the right side of the floor. X3 is trying to defend this
side. 2 is in the right outside lane and 4 has filled the right trailer
lane and by the return pass to 1 should be posted up, *Diagram
2–16*. If X3 is over committing to 2, *Diagram 2–17*, 1 should pass to
4 for the shot. If X3 is committing to 4, *Diagram 2–18*, which is
usually what happens, 1 will pass to 2 for the jumper. If X3 comes
out to stop 2's shot, then 4 will be open down under as in *Diagram
2–19*. 4 should remember to post up as X2 will be coming to defend
him. He should try to keep X2 behind him so that he can easily
receive the pass from 2.

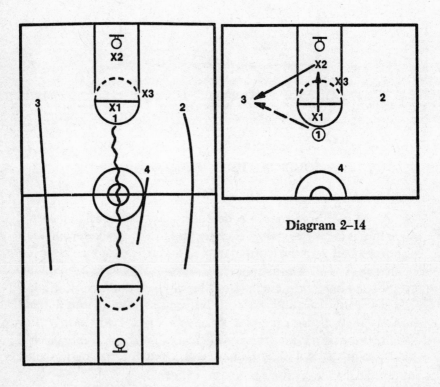

Diagram 2–13

Diagram 2–14

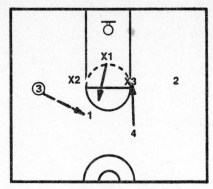

Diagram 2–15

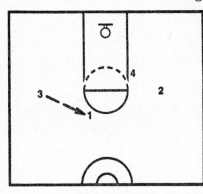

Diagram 2–16

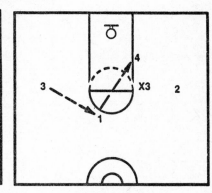

Diagram 2–17

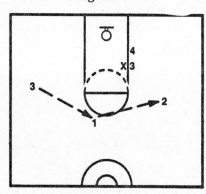

Diagram 2–18

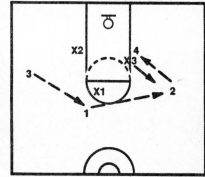

Diagram 2–19

3

FAST BREAKING AFTER
A MISSED FIELD GOAL

The bread 'n butter of the fast break is after an opponent has missed a field goal. In other words, the fast break offense is most potent with good defense. If the ball goes through the basket for the opponent, then the best you can hope is that your fast break can equalize their basket. However, if your defense makes the opponent miss the field goal, then you have an opportunity to make two points to their none.

The year we led the nation in scoring I remember one game in which we started out cold. We were behind 11 points at half time. Within the opponent's next eight possessions in the second half we had made them miss their field goal attempt seven times. We capitalized on all seven of these attempts with our fast break and took the lead for good. It was a vital conference game and one that went a long way in helping us gain the conference championship.

THE TWO GUARD BREAK

The two guard break makes most efficient use of two quick ball handling guards that can score from fifteen feet range. The two guard break allows either of the two guards to receive the outlet pass from the rebounder. We used this type break at Cumberland College the year we led the nation in scoring and were fourth in the nation in the final poll. We were very fortunate to have two guards that had been playing together since junior high school. This is important because in the two guard break each guard needs to know what the other guard is going to do in various situations. This comes by playing together. The more they understand each other the more effective your two guard break will be.

It is very important for the guards to know what lanes they are to cover. When playing man for man defense, the guard defending on the rebound side fills the outside lane on the ball side and stays alert for the outlet pass. The guard away from the rebound should fill the middle lane and be ready for the outlet pass. This situation is shown in *Diagram 3–1* with 1 and 2 being the guards. As you can see, 1, the guard defending on the side the rebound comes off 4's side, takes the outside lane; 2, being the off guard, takes the middle lane. Either one of these can receive the outlet pass in his respective lane in the two guard break.

If the two guards happen to be defending on the same side of the floor, as shown in *Diagram 3–2*, the rule is for the nearest man to the outside lane on the side of the ball to take that lane and the other guard to take the middle. *Diagram 3–3* illustrates this. 1 is nearer the outside lane for that outlet so he fills this lane and 2, farthest from the outside lane on ball side, takes the middle lane. Timing, reading each other, and playing together a lot are important to these techniques.

Most desirable is the outlet pass directly to the middle lane, 4 to 2 in *Diagram 3–4*. But most of the time the outlet pass will go to the outside lane because there is less congestion in this area. When the outlet pass is made to the outside lane, the ball handler should look to pass the ball directly into the middle lane as shown in *Diagram 3–5*. If this pass is not open, the guards perform an "X out." 1 is now to take the ball to the middle lane, and 2 upon seeing this will change lanes with him, taking the outside lane. This "X out" maneuver is shown in *Diagram 3–6*. As you can see, the stress is on getting the ball to the middle of the floor.

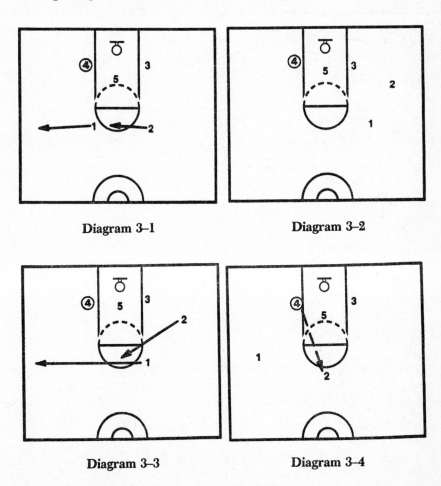

Diagram 3–1

Diagram 3–2

Diagram 3–3

Diagram 3–4

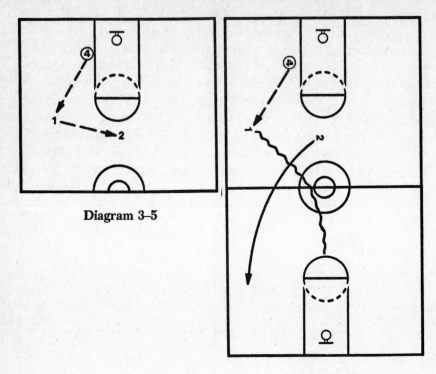

Diagram 3–5

Diagram 3–6

With these two guard techniques described, let us look at the rest of the fast break. Keep in mind, at this point, that the team is in a basic man to man defense. In *Diagram 3–1*, 1 and 2 are the guards, 3 and 4 are the forwards, and 5 is the center. 3, 4, and 5 are always going to rebound defensively because of their position. *Diagram 3–7* illustrates the two guard break with 4 getting the rebound and 1, the guard nearest the outside lane, getting the outlet pass. 2 fills the middle lane and receives the pass from 1. Now either 3 or 5 should fill the other outside lane. The basic rule on filling the outside lane away from the guards is to fill it with a forward and very seldom does the center take this lane. However, a center who can put the 12 to 15 feet jumper in can fill this lane well. In junior high school and high school it would be more appropriate than in college because most of these schools do not have

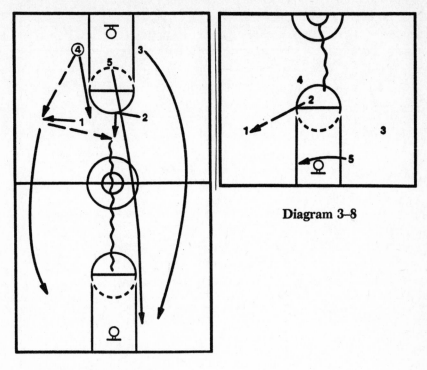

Diagram 3–7

Diagram 3–8

towering big men like those in college. Nevertheless, as in *Diagram 3–7*, 3 fills the outside lane in this situation. Hopefully, 1, 2, and 3 can get a three on one or three on two situation as described in Chapter 2. 5's job, as soon as the rebound starts the fast break, is to fill one of the trailer lanes also described in Chapter 2. He fills either one he wants, left trailer lane in this case, and posts up low provided there was not a layup off the break. As soon as 2 makes a pass to either outside lane in front court, 1 in *Diagram 3–8*, 5 will rebound if he sees a shot is going to be taken by 1; if a shot is not taken, he will post up on ball side looking for a pass from 1. Our rebounding rule on the fast break is that the shooter or passer off the break always acts as a half rebounder, half safety. For example, if 1 shoots the ball he follows to the free-throw line for a long rebound, and if he does not get it or if an opponent gets the ball he acts as a safety on defense. 2, 3, and 5 will be rebounders in this situation. *Diagram 3–9* illustrates 1's assignment of being a half rebounder, half safety. In the two guard break, the rebounder usually fills a safety position. The only time he does not is when a guard rebounds. Upon rebounding the ball and making the outlet pass the safety should stay behind the ball, in case the opponent gets it, until the pass is made from the middle lane to an outside lane in the front court. When this happens he will fill the trailer lane that is open and post opposite the other trailer lane. An example of this is shown in *Diagram 3–10*.

Diagram 3–9

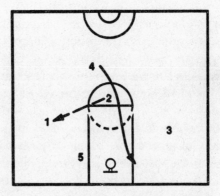

Diagram 3–10

If the players do not get an initial shot, they can turn the ball over to the other side. *Diagram 3–11* shows this. 1, upon seeing he did not have a shot or a pass under for a shot to 5, passes the ball immediately to 2. 2 passes the ball to 3 in the other outside lane and 3 looks to pass to 4 who has posted down low. On this turnover, 5 has the option to hold on the block or come to the high post on ball side. If he does this as in *Diagram 3–12* and receives the pass he can shoot or find the open man. 2 is told to move away from 5 upon his breaking to high post.

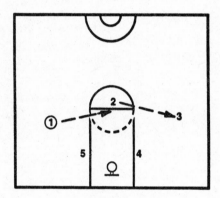

Diagram 3–11

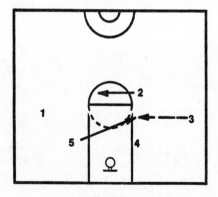

Diagram 3–12

Another technique that can be used in the two guard fast break occurs when a player is slow filling the trailer lane, as in *Diagram 3–13*. As you can see, the three lanes are in a position to score and the trailer lane is slow being filled. When this happens and the pass is made to the outside lane, 1 in *Diagram 3–14*, 3 in the other outside lane can come to the post area in place of 5 if he sees an opening. In this situation, 5 will continue in the trailer lane and go to the block opposite 3. 3's job is to get the ball and score if possible. He also has the option to look to 5 at the other block if he receives the pass from 1, *Diagram 3–15*.

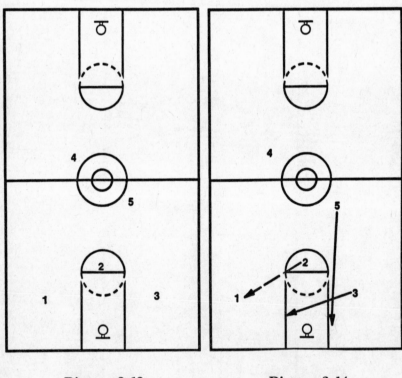

Diagram 3–13   Diagram 3–14

This same technique to the other side is illustrated in *Diagram 3–16*.

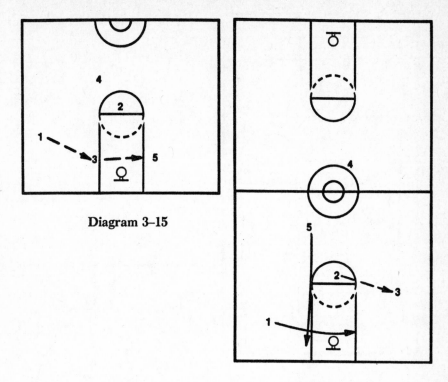

Diagram 3–15

Diagram 3–16

The two guard break also remains the same when 4 gets the rebound and makes the direct outlet pass to 2 in the middle lane. This is illustrated in *Diagram 3–17*. This situation is most desirable. As you can see, the break remains the same. 2 fills the middle lane with the ball, 1 and 3 fill the outside lane, 5 a trailer lane, and 4 is the safety.

If 3, the other forward, gets the rebound, the break is the same as when 4 rebounded and made the outlet pass to 1 or 2 except it is on the other side of the floor. *Diagram 3–18* illustrates using 2 as the outlet. 2 passes to 1 in the middle lane and fills an outside lane. 1 fills the middle lane with the ball. 4 is a forward, and takes the outside lane. 5 is in the trailer lane and 3, the rebounder, is the safety. The break is the same if the outlet were made from 3 to 1 in the middle lane.

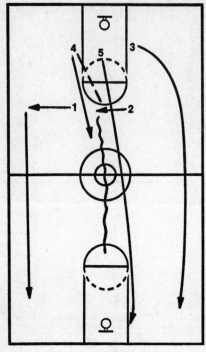

Diagram 3–17

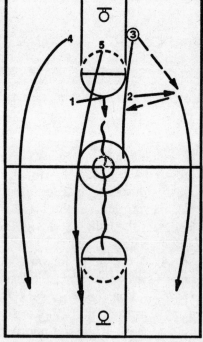

Diagram 3–18

Now let's look at the two guard break when the center 5 rebounds. 1's and 2's assignments are the same, but 3 and 4 have a basic rule in filling the outside lane opposite 1 or 2. That rule is that the first forward that gets to the outside lane has it and the other must take the trailer lane. Usually the forward defensing on the side away from where the rebound is made will get to the outside first. For example, *Diagram 3–19* illustrates the ball coming off for a rebound shading 4's side of the floor with 5, the center, rebounding it. The outlet pass is made to 2 in this case. As you can see, 3 usually will be able to get to the outside lane first.

The entire two guard break with 5, the center, rebounding and making the outlet pass to 2 is shown in *Diagram 3–20*. All the techniques discussed in this chapter thus far apply in this situation.

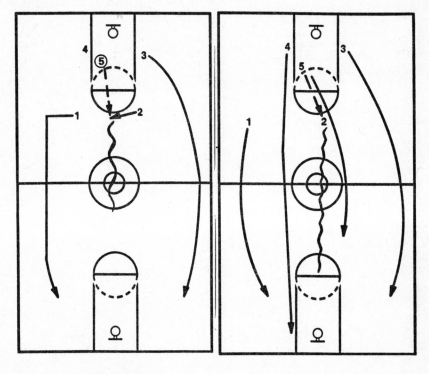

Diagram 3–19   Diagram 3–20

2 fills the middle lane with the ball. 1 and 3 have the outside lane. 4 has taken a trailer lane and 5, the rebounder, is the safety and will stay as the safety until the first pass is made to the outside lane and at that time fills the opposite trailer lane away from 4. The fast break is basically the same when 5 rebounds the ball shading 3's side of the floor, *Diagram 3–21* with 2 receiving the outlet pass. 2 passes to 1 in the middle lane and fills the left outside lane. 4 fills the right outside lane. 3 takes a trailer lane and 5 is the safety.

If 5 should rebound the ball in the center of the floor, both 1 and 2 go to the sideline outlet area to receive this pass, *Diagram 3–22*. Once the outlet has been made to one of the guards, the other guard fills the middle lane. *Diagram 3–23* illustrates the two guard break with 5 rebounding the ball in the center of the floor

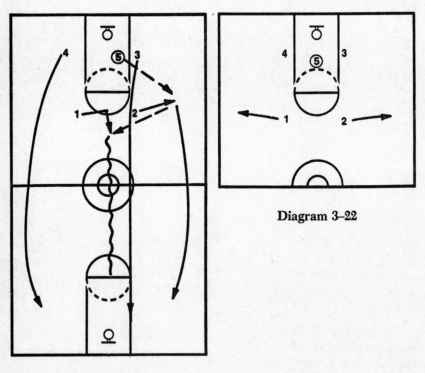

Diagram 3–22

Diagram 3–21

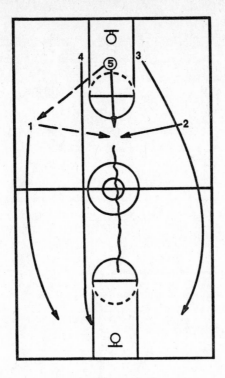

Diagram 3–23

and making the outlet pass to 1. It would be the same basic break if this pass were made to 2. Upon receiving the outlet, 1 passes to 2 in the middle lane and fills the right outside lane. 3 fills the left outside lane. 4 takes a trailer lane and 5 is the safety.

   Diagram 3–24 illustrates the lane filling responsibilities when 1, a guard, gets the rebound from the missed shot by the opponent and dribbles the ball up the floor. When a guard rebounds the ball he has two basic options: one, to dribble the ball up the floor in the middle or outside lane, and two, to make the outlet pass up the floor to the other guard. When a guard rebounds the ball, the other guard comes to the middle of the floor to receive a pass from 1 or perform the X out maneuver that has been described earlier in the chapter. If one advances the ball up the sideline, the sideline break would be in effect. This break is described later in this chapter. In *Diagram 3-24*, 1 fills the middle lane with the dribble and 2 has performed the X out maneuver with him. 3, a forward, should be able to get to the left outside lane first and therefore fills this lane. When a guard rebounds, the forward not filling an outside lane and the center determine who is trailer and who is safety. The first man in a trailer lane gets it and will post up when the pass is made from the middle lane to an outside lane in front court. In this situation 5 has taken the trailer lane and 4 is the safety.

Diagram 3-25 illustrates this same break if 1 makes an advance outlet pass to 2. In this situation the only thing that has changed is 1 taking the right outside lane and 2 the middle lane with the ball.

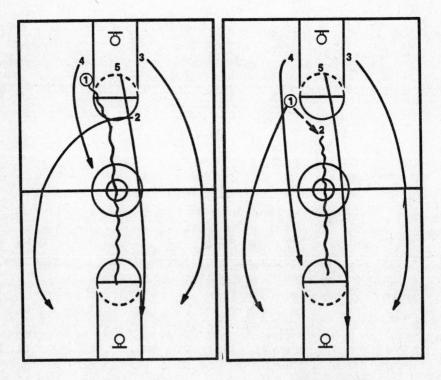

Diagram 3-24

Diagram 3-25

If 2 rebounds the ball all techniques and rules remain the same.

If a team is running the two guard fast break off the 1-2-2 or 1-3-1 zone defense, the techniques also remain the same as described in the chapter. Guards should be in a position where they can be an easy outlet for the rebounders in these defenses.

Diagram 3-26 illustrates the two guard break from the 1-3-1 zone with the 4 man rebounding. Numbers 1 and 2 are the guards; 3 and 4 are the forwards; and 5 is the center. 2 receives the outlet pass and passes to 1, who fills the middle lane with the ball, then fills the left outside lane. 3 is the first forward to get outside so he fills the right outside lane. 4 is the rebounder, and therefore becomes the safety. 5, the center, has trailer lane responsibility.

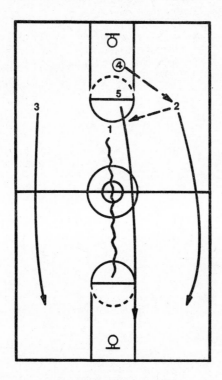

Diagram 3-26

An example of the two guard break from the 1-2-2 zone with the 5 man rebounding is shown in *Diagram 3–27* with 5 rebounding the basketball and making the initial outlet to 1. Numbers 1 and 2 are guards; 3 and 4 are the forwards; 5 is the center. After receiving the outlet pass, 1 passes to 2 and fills the right outside lane. 2 takes the ball down the middle lane for a scoring opportunity. 4 is the first forward to the left outside lane and fills it. 3, the other forward, has the trailer lane responsibility, while 5, the center and rebounder, plays the role of safety.

Zone defenses, as well as man to man defense, provide excellent opportunities to fast break. Placement of the personnel in the zones is the key to the two guard break. The two guard break that has been discussed can be used whether playing against a man to man defense or any type of zone defense.

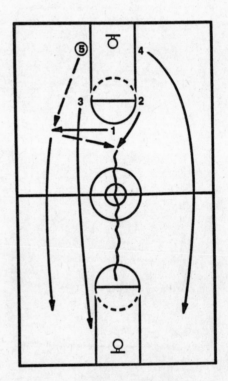

Diagram 3–27

This two guard break that has been illustrated can be used from the 2-3 zone defense. *Diagrams 3–7, 3–17, 3–18, 3–19, 3–20, 3–21, 3–23, 3–24,* and *3–25* specifically show how the two guard fast break would work from the 2-3 zone defense. Techniques remain the same as described in this chapter. How the 2-3 zone defense works will be described in detail in Chapter 6.

SIDELINE BREAK

Because of the congestion in the middle lane area during a fast break there is a need for a sideline break. With five defensive players on the court most of them are going to regroup on defense in this middle lane. When the ball is brought down the middle lane in the fast break there is a lot more pressure on the ball. Therefore, we give our guards the opportunity to use the sideline break which means the ball will be brought up the sideline for the fast break rather than in the middle.

The sideline break has been very productive for my teams over the years. In today's game, scouting has become more prominent and the coaching overall has been exceptional. When opponents prepared for us they sometimes would try to stop us from getting the ball into the middle in the fast break, but by utilizing the sideline break we were still able to get what we wanted off the fast break. One coach that we play against told me after a game that he had stressed to his players all week that they must keep us from breaking up the middle with the ball. They practiced this throughout the week. This team did a pretty good job in stopping the break up the middle, but we saw how open the sideline was and utilized it to our advantage. We won the game 122–82 and the sideline break was the biggest part of our fast break attempts.

The sideline break is similar to the two guard break except that players bring the ball up the sideline rather than in the middle. It can be very effective from man or zone defenses. To simplify matters I am going to show this break using basically the same setup as was illustrated in teaching the two guard break, since the breaks are similar. In *Diagram 3–28*, from a man to man defense, although zones could be used, 1 and 2 are the guards; 3 and 4 are the forwards and 5 the center or post man. *Diagram 3–29* shows 4 getting the rebound and making the outlet pass to 1. 1, upon seeing the middle not open and congested, takes the ball on the dribble up the sideline. The ball handler should use no more than three dribbles and should get to the wing area (free-throw line extended) in three seconds. The wing area is good because it creates a good passing angle. 2 fills the middle lane the same as if he had the basketball, only quicker. 3, because he is the non-rebounding forward, fills the outside lane away from the ball. 5 takes the left trailer lane and reads whether there will be a layup attempt coming

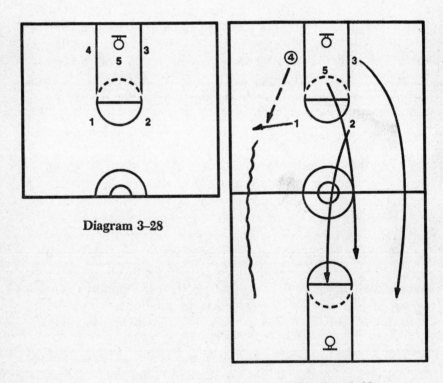

Diagram 3–28

Diagram 3–29

from the initial wave, 1, 2, or 3. If not, his rule is to post up on ball side. 4, the rebounder, is the safety and fills the other trailer lane. His rule is to play safety until the first pass is made and he then goes opposite in the post area of the other trailer.

There are various plays that can be run off the initial wave of the break if an easy shot is not gotten off this initial wave. *Diagram 3–30* shows the "trailer maneuver" off the sideline break, used when the trailers are excellent jump shooters from the key area. The players are using the same setup as in *Diagram 3–29*. The trailer maneuver is great for the sideline break because it usually provides excellent timing for the pass to the trailer. In the trailer maneuver, 1 quickly passes to 2 in the middle lane. 2 flips the ball to 5 coming down the trailer lane for a jump shot. After 5 shoots he

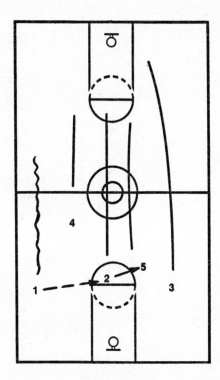

Diagram 3–30

becomes the half rebounder, half safety man. 1, 2, and 3 follow for
the rebound.

Another sideline break situation is shown in *Diagram 3–31*
when 2 instead of stopping in the bubble, continues down the lane
and posts up. As he cuts low to post he is looking for a quick return
pass from 1, *Diagram 3–32*. As 2 posts up, 5 fills the trailer lane at
the block *area opposite* 2. 1 looks to pass to 2 low. If 2 gets the ball,
his options are to shoot or to pass to 5 in the opposite block. 4, upon
seeing 2's maneuver, continues his role as a safety and holds at the
top of the key area. *Diagram 3–33* shows what can be done if 1 does
not have the pass to 2. 1 passes to 4 at the top of the key who passes
the ball to 3. 3 looks to take a quick jumper or pass to 5 posting
down low.

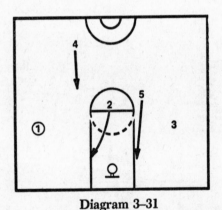

Diagram 3–31

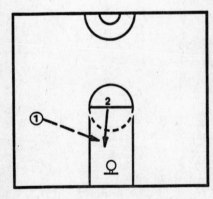

Diagram 3–32

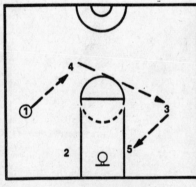

Diagram 3–33

Diagram 3–34 illustrates the sideline break from the rebound off the defense when 5, the center, gets the ball. 1 fills the right outside lane with the ball. 2, the guard without the ball, takes the middle lane. 3 is the nearest forward to the outside lane away from the ball and should get there the quickest, so he takes this lane. 4 takes a trailer lane and posts up if there is no layup attempt. 5 is the safety and fills the opposite trailer lane.

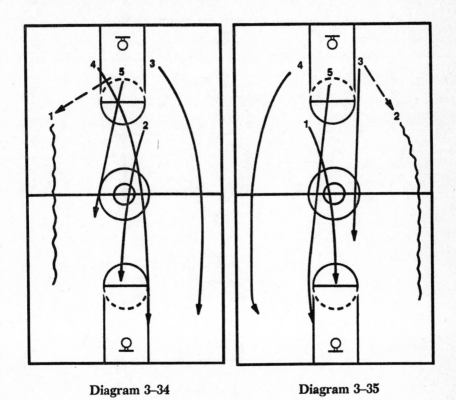

Diagram 3–34   Diagram 3–35

The sideline break is shown on the other side of the floor in *Diagram 3–35* when 3, one of the forwards, gets the rebound. The outlet pass is made to 2 who fills the right outside lane with the ball. 1, the other guard, fills the middle lane. 4, the non rebounding forward, takes the outside lane away from the ball and 3, the rebounder, is the safety and has the trailer lane opposite 5.

If 1 or 2 rebounded the missed shot he would dribble the ball up the sideline if the middle were congested for the sideline break. The sideline break remains the same only there is no outlet. *Diagram 3–36* shows the sideline break with a guard, 1, rebounding the ball in this situation. 1 fills the right outside lane with the ball. 2 takes the middle lane while 3 fills the left outside lane. 5 takes a trailer lane and 4 is the safety.

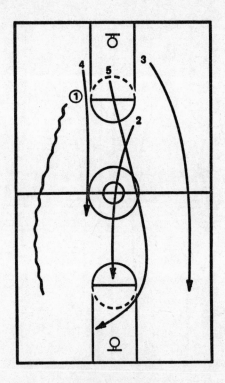

Diagram 3–36

THE CONTROLLED BREAK

The controlled break is the fast break that designates certain lanes to each of the players. No matter where the player is when the ball is rebounded he will have a certain lane he must go to whether it be a middle, outside, or trailer lane. This fast break can be successful when you have a team that has certain characteristics which I shall explain. Most of this system of the controlled break derived from studying the systems used by Sonny Allen at Southern Methodist University and Stu Aberdeen, former assistant coach at the University of Tennessee and now head coach at Marshall University. It is a very effective break when running the point defenses such as the 1-3-1 and 1-2-2 zones. When we run these zones we use the controlled break because of the location of personnel in these defenses.

In the controlled break one man will be designated as the primary ball handler of the break. He is the point guard in the one guard offense or best ball handling guard in the two guard offensive set. He is the best ball handler on the team; he must be quick, unselfish, a good passer, and must be able to hit the jumper from 18 feet and in. He has the middle lane on this break and receives the outlet pass on all fast breaks. Since lanes are designated in the controlled break, players are numbered for each lane. This point guard is the number one man.

The number two man is the second guard. He should also be a good ball handler, quick, a good passer, and able to hit the jumper from the wing and corner. No matter where he is when the rebound comes off to his team, he must fill the right outside lane. He must be in the wing or corner ready to shoot within three seconds providing he does not have a layup.

The number three man is the small forward. His characteristics include being a good rebounder, good passer, and adequate shooter. His job is to always fill the left outside lane.

The number four man in the controlled break is the big forward. He basically fills the left trailer lane. He must be a good rebounder and be able to score from the post area.

The number five man is the post man or center. He fills the right trailer lane and also must score from inside and be a good rebounder.

The trailers are told that they must get to the blocks sprinting so that they can get posted up. From the time the ball is rebounded, there should be a shot within four seconds. The only time the trailers will not sprint directly to the post area is when they see the initial wave, 1, 2, and 3 getting the layup. In this case they hold back.

Diagram 3–37 illustrates the lane filling after the defense has gotten the ball from a rebound for a fast break. The number 1 man is receiving the ball in the bubble area in this example, but is told to go wherever it is necessary to get the ball. Again, in this break no matter where a player is or what he is involved in defensively he must fill his designated lane.

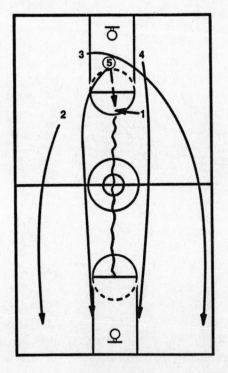

Diagram 3–37

There are various fast break plays that can be run from the controlled break. Diagram 3–38 shows the pop down technique we use off the break. When running this the number 1 man calls out the name "pop" as he crosses the time line signaling this technique. When this happens 2 sets a down screen for 5 and 3 sets a down screen for 4. 1 looks to pass to 4 or 5 at the wing area for a shot or can pass to 2 and 3 inside if they are open. In running this maneuver, 4 and 5 must be adequate jump shooters from outside. If a coach had only one good shooter inside he could run this maneuver to just one side as with 3 and 4 in *Diagram 3–39*.

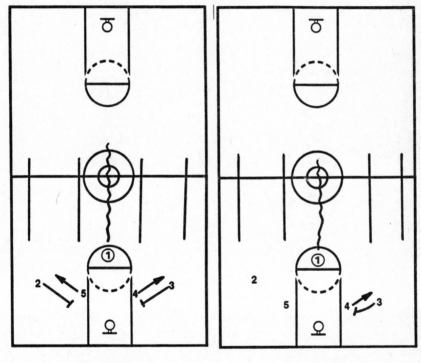

Diagram 3–38   Diagram 3–39

Another technique is the swing maneuver, *Diagram 3–40*, off the controlled break. The number 1 man can signal this by calling out the word "swing." In this situation 4 and 5 try to set a screen on their side for 2 and 3. The 2 and 3 men come off these picks and interchange positions with each other. Hopefully, 1 will have 2 or 3 open for a shot. If they do not have a shot, 2 or 3 look inside at the post area to make a pass.

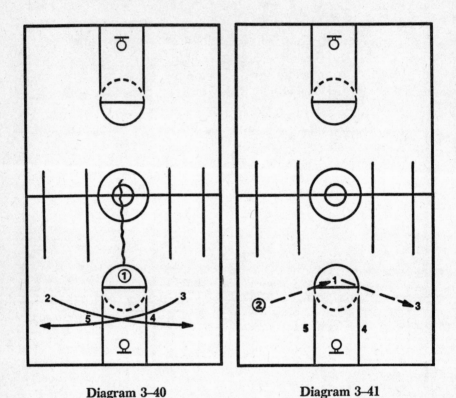

Diagram 3–40   Diagram 3–41

In the controlled break, if there is not a shot off the first pass to the wing or corner, players can turn the ball back to the other side looking for the shot. *Diagram 3–41* illustrates this using 2's side as the initial pass for an example. 2 returns the ball to 1 who passes to 3. 3 can shoot or look inside to 4.

A cross pick maneuver inside, *Diagram 3–42*, works when 1 is returned the ball. The side the ball is passed from, 5 in this case, will receive a cross pick from the opposite block. Thus, when 2 passes to 1, 4 will pick for 5 and execute a reverse pivot. 1 looks to pass to 5 or 4.

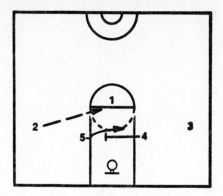

Diagram 3–42

A tremendously strong defensive ball club can allow an early release for the number 2 man at certain times. This comes from the old snowbird technique and it can work. As soon as the ball is shot by the opponent, the number 2 man releases early in hopes of getting a snowbird basket and catching the opponent off guard. This is shown in *Diagram 3-43*. The shot has been taken from the left side and rebounded by 4. He looks to make the long bomb. If he cannot do this he relays the ball to 1 who, hopefully, can make the pass down under, *Diagram 3-44*.

The controlled break is very good when running the 1-3-1 or 1-2-2 zone defenses. The best ball handling guard is placed at the point position defensively, and the others assume their regular lane filling responsibilities.

Diagram 3-45 illustrates an example of the controlled break from the 1-3-1 zone defense with 5, the center, rebounding the ball. The number 1 man is the ball handling guard and plays the point of the zone. He is to go wherever it is necessary to get the outlet pass. The number 2 man is the second guard and plays the baseline of the zone. His job is to fill the right outside lane. The number 3 man, a forward, plays the wing and is responsible for filling the left outside lane. 4, the big forward, plays the left wing and fills the left trailer lane. 5, the center in the 1-3-1 zone, fills the right trailer lane. These lane assignments remain the same no matter which player rebounds the ball.

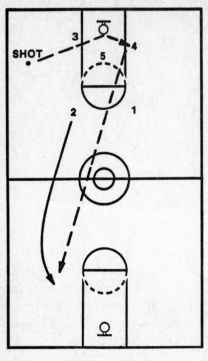

Diagram 3–43

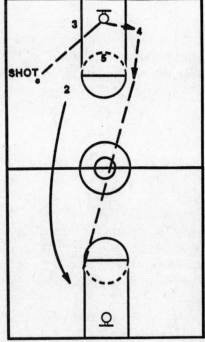

Diagram 3–44

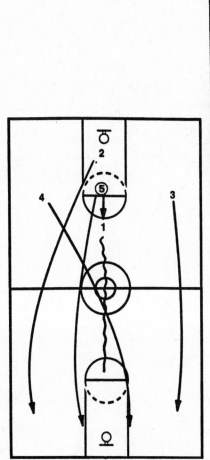

Diagram 3-46

Diagram 3-45

An example of the controlled break from the 1-2-2 zone defense is shown in *Diagram 3-46* with the 4 man rebounding the missed shot. Again, 1 has the middle lane after receiving the outlet; 2 is responsible for the right outside lane; 3, the left outside lane; 4, the left trailer lane; and 5 the right trailer lane.

An illustration of the controlled break from the 2-3 zone that utilizes these same techniques is shown in *Diagram 3-47.*

The controlled break has proven to be successful from both the man and zone defenses by various college and high school coaches throughout the country. The key is placing the right player in the right spot.

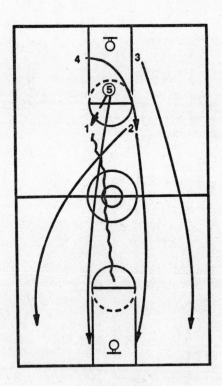

Diagram 3-47

4

FAST BREAKING FOLLOWING
A MADE FIELD GOAL

After seeing the NBA championship series between Boston and Phoenix, I became thoroughly convinced of the advantages of using the fast break after a made field goal by an opponent. The fast break after a made field goal puts a lot of pressure on the defense by making the team regroup in a hurry. If one player on the defensive team loafs while regrouping, the fast break should be successful. A team that utilizes this type of fast break has to be in condition because they will be running an entire game. Recent NBA championship series showed that the pros, who are grown men, can run an entire game even though the pros play longer than anyone. The college and high school players are younger than the pros and do not have to play as long and this should be an advantage to them

and should show coaches at this level that it can be done successfully. In essence, if the pros can do it, other systems can do it.

The fast break after a made field goal is one phase of the game
that coaches do not stress enough. Coaches should use it more to
their advantage to put pressure on the defense, when they are a
quicker team, when they are in better condition than the opponent, when they need to get momentum going.

Fast breaking can provide at least as much momentum as any
other phase of the game. A successful fast break after a made field
goal can give you momentum because it is usually a quick basket
that has retaliated against the opponent's previous score.

POST MAN TECHNIQUE

The post man technique is a very big part of the fast break
following a successful field goal by the opponent. When the ball
goes through the basket for a score, a post man brings the ball
in-bounds for the fast break. The reason for this is that defensively
he is usually in the basket area and closest to the ball when it comes
through the net for a score more often than anyone else. He is also
one of the bigger players on the team and can see the floor over
opponents that guard him better. He is usually one of the stronger
players and can make the length-of-the-court pass with relative
ease. Of course, it is necessary to establish drills to maintain accuracy when making this pass. The primary drill we use is shown in
Diagram 4–1. A manager shoots from the free-throw line. 1 gets
the ball immediately as it falls through the basket, steps out of
bounds, and fires the ball the length of the floor to 2.

This brings me to an important coaching point, bringing the
ball in-bounds. We do not want the passer bringing the ball in-
bounds to stand under the goal because this limits his passing area.
When a passer establishes this position there is no way he can make
a length of the floor pass. He has limited his passing to the back
court. When he does this he not only limits the passing, but

makes it very advantageous to a team that applies pressure in the
back court. Pressing teams can gamble by bringing all of the pres-
sers in the back court to try for a steal on the in-bounds pass
without losing anything.

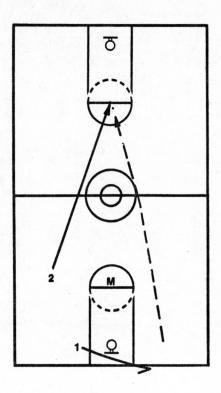

Diagram 4–1

We also tell the post man that brings the ball in not to use a
square stance unless there is pressure in the back court on the
in-bound pass. The reason for this is that with the square stance he
cannot pass the ball as far up the court as with the stance of the
baseball pass described in Chapter 1. The baseball pass is usually
the pass we want to make when there is no back court pressure.

It is necessary that the post man be able to find all of his
teammates when bringing the ball in-bounds. He must get the ball

and be able to see all of the floor because different people will be open for the pass throughout various parts of the game.

Quickness in getting the ball out of bounds to make the in-bounds pass after a made basket is one of the biggest keys to a successful fast break in this situation. The post man must react quickly and must be drilled to perfection in getting this pass in-bounds quickly. The fast break after a made field goal loses about 5 feet in area, *Diagram 4–2*, to the fast break after a missed field goal making the quickness in which the ball is brought in-bounds the big factor in making up for the lost ground caused by a made basket.

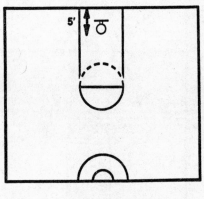

Diagram 4–2

THE "JAGUAR" BREAK AND EARLY OFFENSE

The "Jaguar" Break is named after the University of South Alabama Jaguars. It is used after a successful field goal by the opponent. It stresses getting the ball in-bounds quickly and moving the ball up the floor as fast as possible. This break attempts to counteract the score the opponent just made. This break is primarily effective when teams are playing man-to-man defense in the front court. An early offense that will be described later is part of the Jaguar Break.

In the Jaguar Break, players are numbered as in the controlled break. The number 1 man is the ball handling guard and is the primary receiver for the in-bounds pass. The number 2 man is the second guard and fills the right outside lane. The number 3 man is the small forward and fills the left outside lane. The number 4 man is a post man and goes directly to the low post block on either side of the floor. The number 5 man is the in-bounds passer.

The basic Jaguar Break is shown in *Diagram 4–3* from a hypothetical defensive situation. 5 brings the ball out of bounds for the pass as quickly as possible, looking deep for any cheap basket that might have developed. He then looks to 1, the primary receiver. Because of the congestion and flow of traffic down the middle of the floor after a made basket, we tell 1 to work to receive the ball at the sideline. He works from within the hash mark area to the passer to receive the ball. When he receives the ball he primarily will fill the middle lane with the ball looking to score or pass the ball to 2, 3, or 4 in their respective lanes for a score.

When 2 or 3 get the ball from 1 they look for the easy jumper and for 4 down low, *Diagram 4–4*.

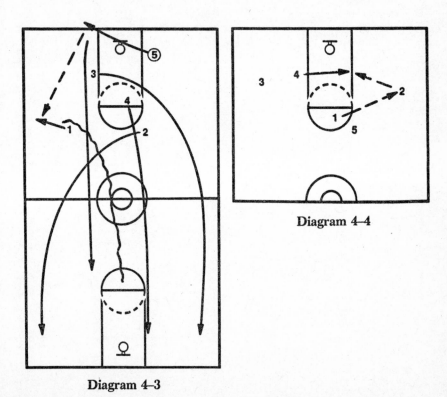

Diagram 4–4

Diagram 4–3

An automatic interchange will occur in the Jaguar Break when 2 or 3 do not have a scoring situation. This is illustrated in *Diagram 4–5*. As 1 gets to the bubble in the front court and there is no pass to 2, 3, or 4 on the initial wave, 2 and 3 will criss-cross and look for the pass. When the pass to the wing is made, 5, who is a safety until the first pass is made in the front court, establishes high post position on the ball side. Upon this pass, using 2 as an example, 1 pops back to the top of the key, *Diagram 4–6*, and the break now has the look shown in *Diagram 4–7*. 1, the ball handler is at the top of the key; 2, the second guard is at the left wing area; 3, the small forward is at the right wing area; 4 and 5, the post men, are at the respective high and low post areas.

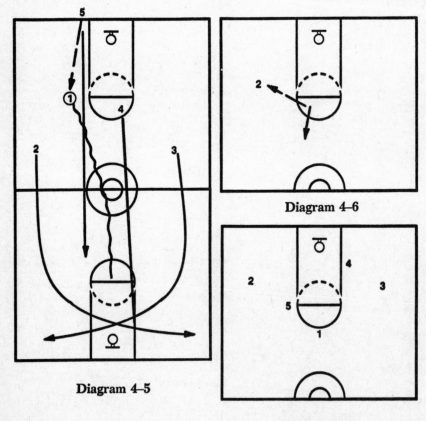

Diagram 4–5

Diagram 4–6

Diagram 4–7

At this point, this break becomes an early offense that has rules, for the most part by Dr. Glenn Wilkes of Stetson University. The early offense is a passing game from the break situation developed in *Diagram 4–7*. It limits dribbling and requires a lot of movement on the part of the fast break team. The philosophy of the early offense and Jaguar Break is that the team moves down the floor quickly when it gets the ball and continues to move and tries to score once it gets to the front court. Doing this successfully keeps the team from having to set up for pattern play and keeps the defense from getting set.

This fast break early offense is broken into three areas that are listed below. The general rules are used by every offensive man on the floor. The perimeter rules are used by our 1, 2, and 3 man. The post play rules are used by the 4 and 5 man.

General Rules

1. You must move every time a pass is made.
2. Look to pass first, shoot second, and drive third. (Think pass)
3. No more than 2 dribbles after offense is initiated.
4. Must make at least 4 passes before shot is taken.
5. Every third pass must go to a post man.
6. Anytime you're overplayed, cut to the goal or screen for a teammate.
7. Always make the *easy* pass.
8. After receiving the pass, face the goal, and hold the ball at least 2 seconds before you pass (give things a chance to develop inside).
9. Offensive movement begins when the ball crosses midcourt area against any pressure.

Post Play Rules

1. High post man ball side, low post man away from the ball.

2. Take the ball to the goal if at all possible . . . be conscious of drawing the foul pump faking.

3. When you receive the pass, look for splitting action and backdoor action by the perimeter players.

4. Ball passed to high post—look inside (low post) and then to the weakside.

5. Ball passed to low post—look to score first, to high post man going down the lane second, and a perimeter player third.

Perimeter Play Rules

1. When you pass the ball: A) cut to the goal (may turn out either way) B) screen away from the ball C) look to screen down (someone below you).

2. Ball is passed to post: A) screen closest player or cut to open spot.

3. Feed the ball inside with a low pass (knee high).

In the Jaguar Break, if the number 1 man decides that he wants to bring the ball up the sideline after receiving the in-bounds pass, the break will look as shown in *Diagram 4-8, 4-9,* and *4-10.* As you can see this is a set break. When 1 brings the ball up the sideline on the right side of the floor, 2 will clear to the left side of the floor. 3 will flash into the low post area on the ball side of the floor from his left outside lane. The team is looking to take the ball inside to 3 at this low post area, *Diagram 4-9,* with 2 and 4, who has filled the offside low post, rebounding any missed shot. If 3 is not open, 1 will swing the ball out front to the safety man 5, *Diagram 4-10,* and at this point 4 will set a stacked double screen with number 3. 5 then passes the ball to 2 who has cleared to this area. 1 will break off the double pick set by 3 and 4 and receive the pass from 2, *Diagram 4-11.*

The timing of these picks and maneuvers is of utmost importance. A coach should make sure his team spends plenty of practice time on these fundamentals to insure proper execution.

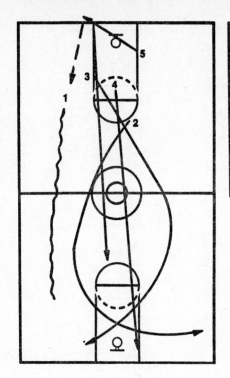

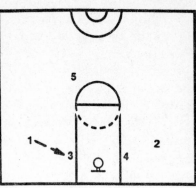

Diagram 4–9

Diagram 4–8

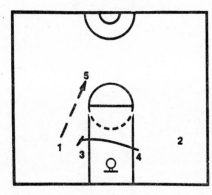

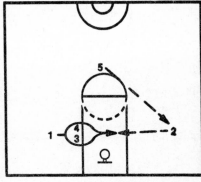

Diagram 4–10

Diagram 4–11

This break is shown when 1 brings the ball up the sideline in 3's lane on the left side of the floor in *Diagrams 4–12, 4–13,* and *4–14.* In *Diagram 4–12,* 3 is now the man who clears to the opposite side of the floor when 1 comes up his sideline. 2 now becomes the flasher at the low post area on the ball side of the floor. 4 fills the offside low post area and 5 is the safety man. If the 2 man is not open or there is no score in this initial wave, 1 will swing the ball out front to 5, *Diagram 4–13,* and 2 and 4 set the double pick. 5 then passes the ball to 3, and 1 comes off the double pick looking for a pass from 3 for a score, *Diagram 4–14.*

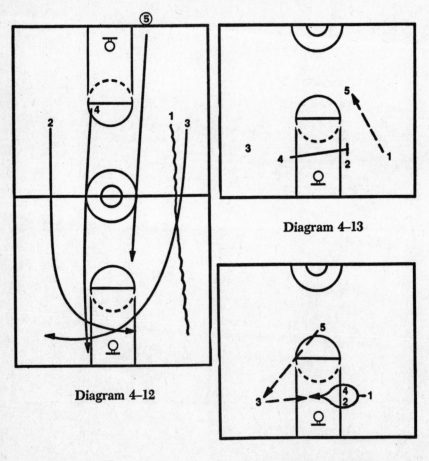

Diagram 4–12

Diagram 4–13

Diagram 4–14

FAST BREAKING AGAINST MAN TO MAN
FULL COURT PRESSURE

I have always felt that to be a consistently good fast breaking team you must be able to fast break against teams that apply back court pressure as well as front court pressure. I know of many coaches who would rather not fast break against full court pressure. This causes a lack of consistency in the break and could show to the players a lack of confidence in them to break against all situations.

There are certain times when a team cannot fast break against full court pressure. These situations can occur when a net hangs up on the goal after a made basket and the official has to call time out or the ball, upon coming out of the net, hits a player and dribbles out of bounds. These are a couple of examples and there are others, but basically a team should be able to fast break against full court pressure 90 percent of the time if it should choose to do so.

Our basic fast break against man to man full court pressure is the same as shown in *Diagram 4–3*, but there are certain techniques that the number 1 man, the primary in-bounds receiver, must be taught. These techniques occur when number 1's man is trying to deny the in-bounds pass, *Diagram 4–15*, from the 5 man. The defensive man is fronting number 1 and does not want him getting the ball. There are two techniques that are important to 1 to free himself to get the ball. We call these the V cut technique and the "pin" technique.

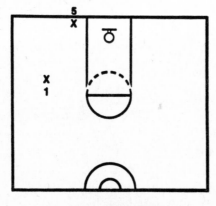

Diagram 4–15

The V cut technique is shown in *Diagrams 4–16* and *4–17*. In this technique the 1 man takes his man one way and after 3 to 4 steps cuts back the other way making what looks like a V cut to get the ball. The purpose of this maneuver is to make the defensive man commit with you one way and when you have him committed cut in the opposite direction freeing yourself for the ball. Quick, sharp cuts are necessary for the 1 man to get the ball off the V cut technique.

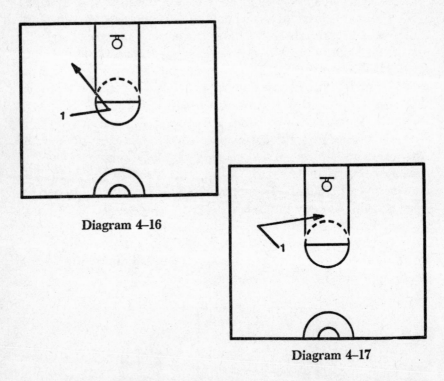

Diagram 4–16

Diagram 4–17

The "pin" technique, *Diagrams 4–18* and *4–19*, is also very effective against overplay on the in-bounds technique. In the pin technique 1 takes the denying defensive man directly to the end line out of bounds, *Diagram 4–18*. Now, if the defensive man still denies, all 1 has to do is pin him on his back as if he were blocking off for a rebound and 5 can make an easy toss to 1, *Diagram 4–19*, and 1 should be off to the races.

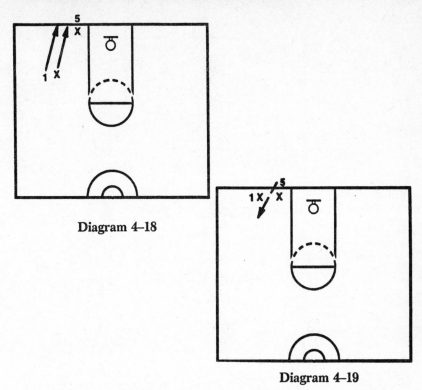

Diagram 4–18

Diagram 4–19

Once the V cut technique or pin technique is executed and 1 gets the ball, the same fast break is on as shown in *Diagram 4–3*.

When there is man to man full court pressure the number 2 man, the second guard, becomes the secondary receiver for the in-bounds pass from number 5. There will be times when he will receive the in-bounds pass, and when this happens, 2 and 1 will swap assignments and the fast break will look as shown in *Diagram 4–20*. Number 2 is now the in-bounds receiver and fills the middle lane with the ball. The 1 man, who normally has the middle lane, now has the right outside lane. 3 fills the left outside lane. 4 takes the low post on either side of the floor. 5, the in-bounds passer, is the safety man and fills the post area opposite 4 once the first pass is made from the 2 man in the front court.

If 2 brings the ball up the sideline the team will use the same break illustrated in *Diagrams 4–8* and *4–12*. 2 and 1 swap assignments in this situation.

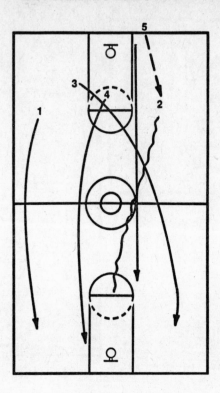

Diagram 4–20

FAST BREAKING AGAINST BACK COURT ZONE PRESSURE

I am an advocate of the zone press as evidenced by my previous book entitled *Zone Press Variations for Winning Basketball*. Zone presses are effective defensive weapons and can disrupt fast breaks if a team is not careful. Zone presses usually trap in four areas. The two areas shaded in *Diagram 4–21* are the areas where traps or double teams are usually made with full court zone presses. *Diagram 4–22* shows the areas where traps usually occur from three-quarter court zone presses in the back court.

Zone presses usually occur after a made basket and in these situations a team can use the fast break shown in *Diagram 4–3*.

When facing zone presses teams must remember that they must get the ball in-bounds quickly and try to beat the double teams wherever they occur in the back court. If a team accomplishes this it will have a very advantageous fast break opportunity against the defense. An example of this is shown in *Diagram 4–23* with the ball being brought in quickly enough to break a double team in the back court. There should at least be a 4 on 3 fast break situation. Using X1 and X2 as trappers from a 1-2-1-1 full court zone press, it is evident that if 1 can get through the trap as the illustration shows the odds are in the offensive team's favor.

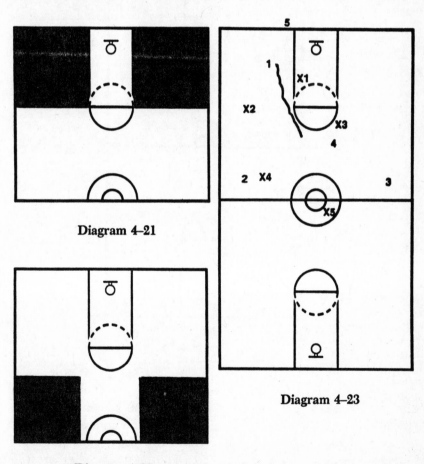

Diagram 4–21

Diagram 4–22

Diagram 4–23

If a team is trapping in the three quarter court area, *Diagram 4-22*, the philosophy remains the same. The only thing a team wants to do differently is make a deeper in-bounds pass, *Diagram 4-24*. Since the defense is dropping back, this pass should be no problem. Again, a coach needs to stress getting the ball up the floor so quickly that the team will not give the double team a chance to develop.

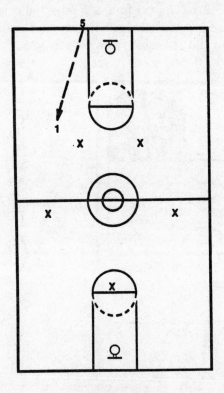

Diagram 4-24

If for some reason the defense does get the double team on the ball handler in the fast break, a team must keep three basic principles in mind with the other receivers. There are three basic areas that the passer in the trap can throw against the full court zone press and they are shown in *Diagram 4-25*. They are the sideline pass, the middle pass, and the back pass. A fourth area is shown in *Diagram 4-26*, and this is the deep area, but this pass should be thrown only if a man is completely wide open and this will not be very often. These pass areas basically exist for the passer in a trap against three quarter court presses.

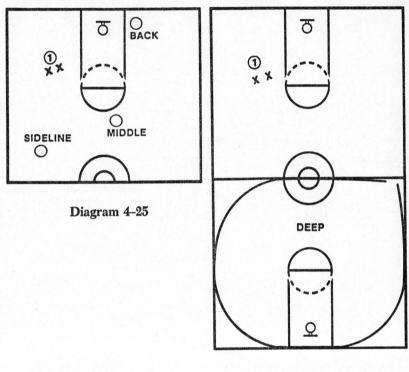

Diagram 4-25

Diagram 4-26

So, from our break, *Diagram 4-3*, players must be alert from their lanes to be receivers in these areas. When 1 is trapped in the break on the right side of the floor, the 2 man who fills the right outside lane is responsible for the sideline pass behind the seam of the double team. The number 3 man, who fills the left outside lane, will be able to receive the deep passes. The number 4 man will normally be heading for the blocks in the middle lane and will always be responsible for helping in the middle pass area and our number 5 man, the in-bounds passer, is always behind the ball as a safety and is responsible for a back pass.

From these areas let us look at the fast break situations that should occur. In each situation, once the pass is completed the fast breaking team has the odds to score in its favor.

Diagram 4–27 illustrates the break when 1 makes the sideline pass to 2 against a full court zone press. A 3 on 2 situation should occur against the two back men in the press and someone should get a layup. If not, 4 will post up on a block. 1 after making the pass to 2 fills the right outside lane and 2 looks to pass to him, *Diagram 4–28*. 1 looks to shoot or pass low to 4 on the block. 5 fills the low post area opposite the number 4 man.

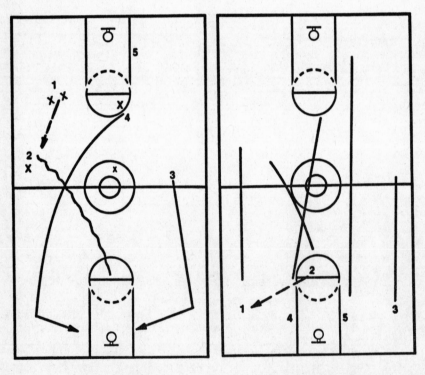

Diagram 4–27   Diagram 4–28

This same technique can occur with 1 passing to 3 in the left outside lane. He can also take the jumper or pass low to 5 at the low post area.

Diagram 4–29 illustrates the pass out of the trap from number 1 to number 4 in the middle area against a full court zone press. If 4 is a good enough ball handler, he can bring the ball down the middle for the 3 on 2 situation. If he does, 1 and 5 stay behind the ball as trailers and safety men. If there is no layup, 4 can pass to either lane, 2 in this case, *Diagram 4–30.* When this happens 4 slides down the lane in his normal low post position. 5 takes the opposite low post area. 1 is in the middle lane for a return pass and 3 is in the left outside lane. 2 looks to hit number 4 immediately for a return pass, *Diagram 4–31.* If there is nothing here we can go to our offense from this point.

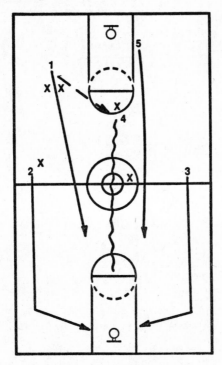

Diagram 4–29

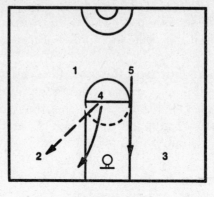

Diagram 4–30

Diagram 4–31

Diagram 4–32 illustrates the break attempt when the pass is made from 1 to 4 against the full court trap and 4 is not a good ball handler. In this situation 2 makes a diagonal cut in front of 4 and receives the pass. 1 fills the right outside lane and 3 the left outside lane. 4 and 5 stay behind the ball until the first pass is made in the front court, at which time they will post up at the low post area on both sides of the floor.

Diagram 4–33 shows the fast break attack when the back pass is made from 1 to 5 against a full court zone press. We do not want 5 putting the ball on the floor. Therefore 3 is told he must do whatever is necessary to receive the ball. 2 is instructed to make a diagonal cut from his outside lane position to an opening in the middle of the floor and receive the pass from 3. 2, upon receiving the pass, has the middle lane, 3 the left outside lane, and 1 the right outside lane. 4 and 5 stay behind the ball until the first pass is made to the wing area in front court at which time they will post up at the blocks.

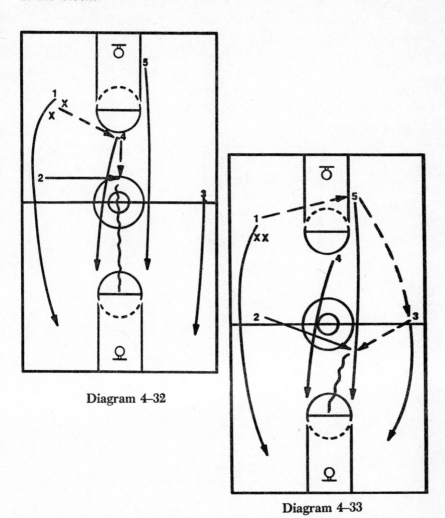

Diagram 4–32

Diagram 4–33

If 3 cannot hit 2 for the diagonal pass he takes the middle, *Diagram 4–34*, and 2 takes the left outside lane and the break will still remain the same except for the fact that these two are swapping assignments.

These fast break situations against back court zone presses can annihilate the defense. Nothing dejects a press more than a quick basket against the press. Players get down on their defense and it sometimes has a negative effect on other parts of their game.

When choosing a system to use against the back court zone press, it is suggested that the coach develop a philosophy of beating the press quickly by fast breaking the press.

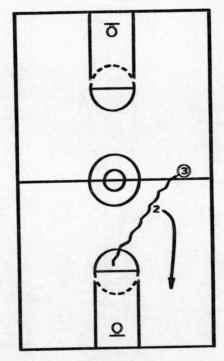

Diagram 4–34

5

FAST BREAKING FROM
THE FREE-THROW LINE

Sending the opponent to the free-throw line gives him the opportunity for an easy score. The free-throw allows the opponent to shoot the ball without defensive pressure. Of course, teams want the least number of fouls possible because they do not want to be beaten by the free-throw. When a team puts the opponent to the free-throw line by fouling him on defense, it has committed a mistake. To overcome the mistake a team should fast break after any made or missed free-throw. If the team can get a basket back off the free-throw fast break, it has evened out the mistake. So many times I have seen teams lose their composure by constant fouls that send the opponent to the free-throw line. They become dejected, lose insight into other parts of the game, and eventually get beaten. Therefore, it has always been our feeling that we must have the philosophy of running after any made or missed free-throw. I sincerely believe that it has helped us win many basketball games over the years.

THE MISSED FREE-THROW

On all free-throw situations in which the opponent is at the free-throw line the fast breaking team can line up as shown in *Diagram 5-1*. The number 1 man is the best ball handler; the 2 man is the second guard and has the responsibility of blocking out the shooter; the 3 man is the smallest forward; 4 is the biggest forward; and 5 is the center and should be the best rebounder.

There are two very good methods to use on the missed free-throw fast break. If the number 4 man can run well and hit the 12 to 15 feet jumper, one break will work, and if a team does not have an ideal man in the number 4 spot, another type will work.

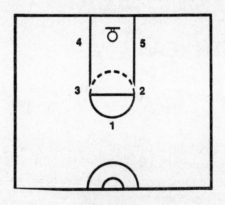

Diagram 5–1

The fast break to utilize with an ideal man who can run from the number 4 spot is illustrated in *Diagram 5–2* with 5, the center, rebounding the missed free-throw attempt. 5 makes the pass to the 2 man who is being a relay man to get the ball to 1, the best ball handler. 1 has made a diagonal cut to 2 at the sideline and upon receiving the ball fills the middle lane. 3 has the responsibility of taking the left outside lane and 4 has the right outside lane. 2 and 5 stay behind the ball and act as safeties. When 1 gets to the free-throw line 2 has stayed behind the ball and to the right side of the ball handler and 5 is to the left, *Diagram 5–3*. If a score does not occur from the initial wave, 4 posts up in the low post area on his side, 2 fills the right side, 5 takes the post opposite 4, and 3 remains in the left outside lane, illustrated in *Diagram 5–4*. Now the team is ready to run our offense or any set technique off the fast break as described in previous chapters.

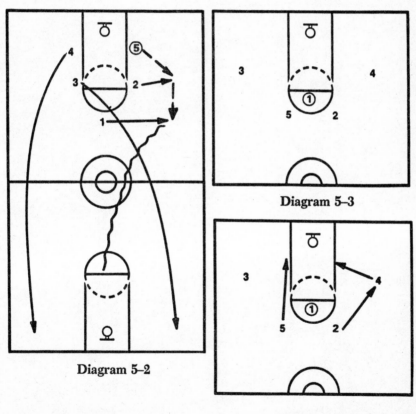

Diagram 5–2

Diagram 5–3

Diagram 5–4

Diagram 5–5 illustrates the fast break when 4 gets the rebound off the missed free-throw attempt. 3 acts as the relay man on
this side of the floor and receives the outlet pass from 4. 1 makes a
diagonal cut to 3 and receives the pass from him and fills the
middle lane with the ball. The 2 man has the responsibility of filling
the right outside lane and 4 fills the opposite left outside lane. 3
and 5 stay behind the ball, 3 to the left of 1 and 5 to the right, until
they see they will not get a score from the initial wave, *Diagram
5–6*. When this happens, the same rotating technique illustrated in
Diagram 5–4 is used. 4 posts up low on his side, 3 fills the left side,
5 takes the post opposite 4, and 2 remains in the right outside lane.

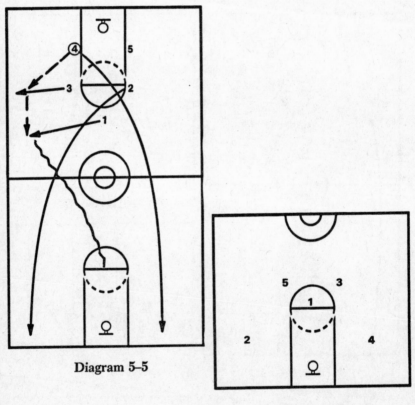

Diagram 5–5

Diagram 5–6

Diagram 5–7 illustrates this missed free-throw fast break when the 3 man rebounds the ball. When this happens the outlet will be made to 1 at the sideline area. 1 fills the middle lane with the ball. 2 fills the right outside lane and 4 has the left outside lane. 3 and 5 stay behind the ball, 3 to the left of 1 and 5 to the right, *Diagram 5–8.* If a score does not come from 1, 2, or 4 on the initial wave, 4 posts up at the block on his side, 5 goes to the opposite post area, and 3 fills the left outside lane. This is shown in *Diagram 5–9.* They are now ready to run their offense or any set fast break technique.

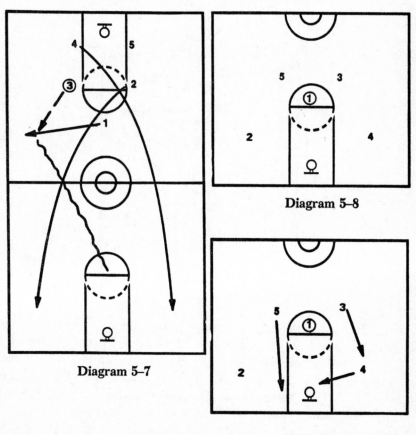

Diagram 5–7

Diagram 5–8

Diagram 5–9

The fast break when 2 gets the rebound off the missed free-throw is shown in *Diagram 5–10*. It is basically the same break as when 3 rebounded, but there are different assignments. 2 rebounds and makes the outlet pass to 1. 1 fills the middle lane, 3 the left outside lane, and 4 the right outside lane. 2 and 5 stay behind the ball, 2 to the right of the ball handler and 5 to the left.

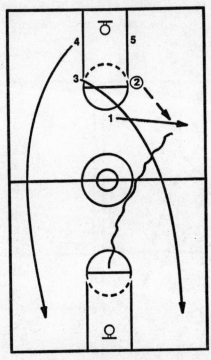

Diagram 5–10

The fast break that can be used when the number 4 man is not effective filling an outside lane is shown in *Diagram 5–11* with 5 rebounding the missed free-throw. This is a controlled break situation. 2 receives the outlet pass from 5, passes to 1 up the sideline, and fills the left outside lane. 1, upon receiving the pass, fills the middle lane and 3 takes the right outside lane. 4's responsibility is to get to the most vulnerable post area. His only rule is not to interfere with a layup that might occur from 1, 2, or 3. 5 stays behind the ball until the first pass is made in the front court at which time he fills the post area opposite 4.

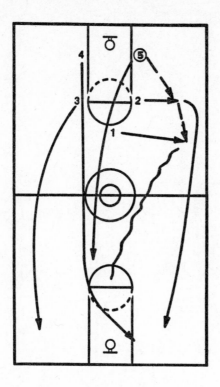

Diagram 5-11

The same technique occurs when 4 rebounds the missed free-throw, *Diagram 5–12*. All lanes are filled the same as when 5 rebounded. The only difference when 4 rebounds is that the 3 man becomes the relay man for the 1 man.

The break also remains the same when 3 or 2 rebounds the missed free-throw attempt. *Diagram 5–13* illustrates the fast break when 3 rebounds the missed free-throw, and *Diagram 5–14* illustrates the fast break when 2 rebounds the missed free-throw. As you can see, the only change is that there is no relay pass to 1 as when 4 or 5 rebounds.

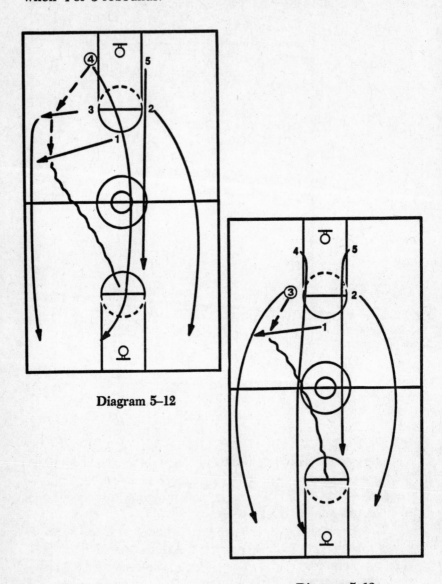

Diagram 5–12

Diagram 5–13

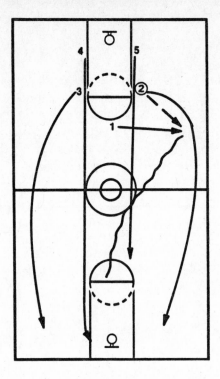

Diagram 5–14

THE MADE FREE-THROW

The alignment for the made free-throw fast break is illustrated in *Diagram 5–1*. A simple numbering system can be used to tell the players what type fast break to run if the free-throw is made. Before the opponent goes to the free-throw line the number 1 man designates the type of fast break play the team is going to run if the free throw is made.

For example, if the number 1 man calls out the number one to the other players, they run the fast break illustrated in *Diagram 5–15*. 5, the center, is the in-bounds passer and passes to 3. In this fast break, 2 makes a diagonal cut to 3 and receives the pass and fills the middle lane with the ball. 1, upon seeing the free-throw go through the basket, releases to the right outside lane. 4 has the responsibility of filling the left outside lane. 3 and 5 stay behind the ball, 3 to the left of 2 and 5 to the right, *Diagram 5–16*. If there is no layup by 1, 2, or 4, 4 posts up on his side. 3 then fills the left outside lane, and 5 posts up opposite 4. This is shown in *Diagram 5–17*. 2 can now pass to 3 or 1 at the wings, *Diagram 5–18*, or to 4 or 5 inside, *Diagram 5–19*. If 3 or 1 do not have the jumper when they receive the pass, they look low to 4 or 5.

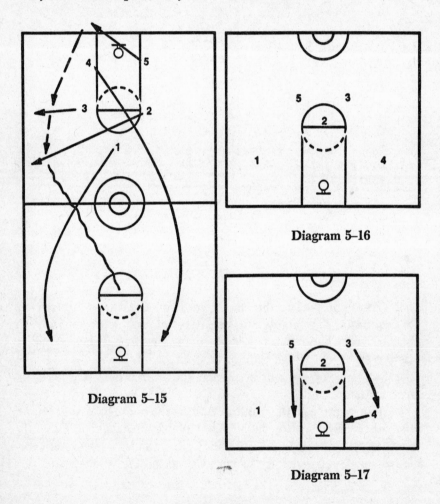

Diagram 5–15

Diagram 5–16

Diagram 5–17

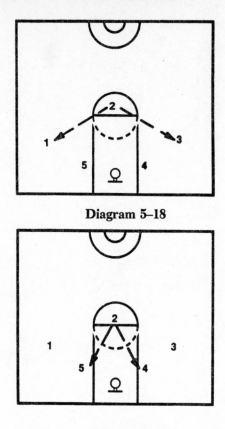

Diagram 5–18

Diagram 5–19

Another break off the made free-throw, possibly designated as the number two break, is shown in *Diagram 5–20*. In this break, 4 is the in-bounds passer. 5 is a relay man to pass the ball after receiving the in-bounds pass to 1. 1 receives the relay pass and fills the middle lane with the ball looking up the floor to pass to 2 or 3 for a layup. 2 and 3 make what looks like an X maneuver. 2 fills the right lane from the left side of the free-throw line and 3 fills the left lane from the right side of the free-throw line. 4 and 5 have the responsibility of going to the low post area in the front court once the first pass is made in front court. The one that gets to either of the blocks first has that block and the other man takes the other post. An

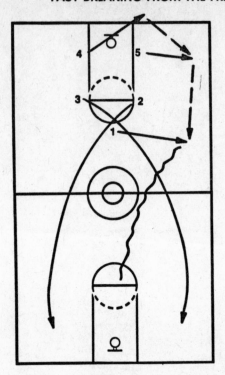

Diagram 5-20

example of this is shown in *Diagram 5-21*. 4 gets to the ball side block first and takes this post area and anticipates a pass from 3. 5 has filled the opposite block.

When the number 1 man calls another number, say number three, the team can use the break illustrated in *Diagram 5-22*. This is a controlled break used as a change up of breaks or as compensation for a lack of exceptional ball handlers. 5 takes the ball out of the basket and in-bounds the ball to 1. 1 fills the middle lane with the ball and looks up the floor to hit 2, who has taken the right outside lane, or 3, who has filled the left outside lane, for the layup. 4 should be the first big man down and takes either low post area. 5 is the safety man until the first pass is made in the front court and at this time will fill the low post opposite 4.

Diagram 5–21

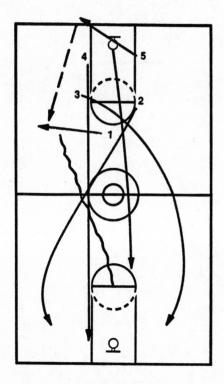

Diagram 5–22

This same break can be run to the other side with 4 bringing the ball in-bounds as in *Diagram 5–23*. This can be signalled by calling the number four.

The number five and six breaks here are fast break situations used by C. M. Newton, head basketball coach at the University of Alabama. He was very successful with this when he had All-American Leon Douglas. These breaks can be used when the team has an exceptional center who can get down the floor quickly and is an exceptional scorer from the low post area. Both breaks are quick plays with quick passes and *they must be executed quickly*. In the first break 4 gets the ball out of the basket and, as shown in *Diagram 5–24*, makes the in-bounds pass to 2. 2 passes to 1 up the sideline and he dribbles the ball down the left outside lane. 5, the center, has the responsibility of getting to the ball side low post as quickly as possible. The goal is to get the ball inside from 1 to 5 in the low post area for a score.

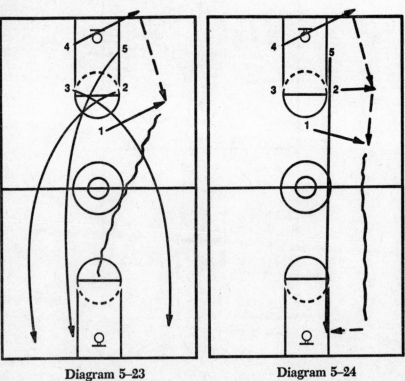

Diagram 5–23   Diagram 5–24

The other of these two breaks is to the other side and is run when the number 4 man executes this technique. It is illustrated in *Diagram 5–25*.

A number seven break is a different type alignment used for the fast break after a made free-throw as shown in *Diagram 5–26*. This particular fast break is illustrated in *Diagram 5–27*. 5 is the inbounds passer and throws the ball to 2. 1 is to receive the pass from 2 near the hash mark area in front court. Upon receiving the pass he dribbles to the basket looking for 3 who has posted low from the free-throw line area in the front court.

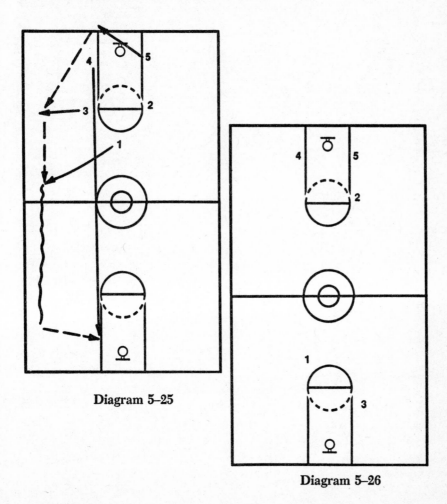

Diagram 5–25

Diagram 5–26

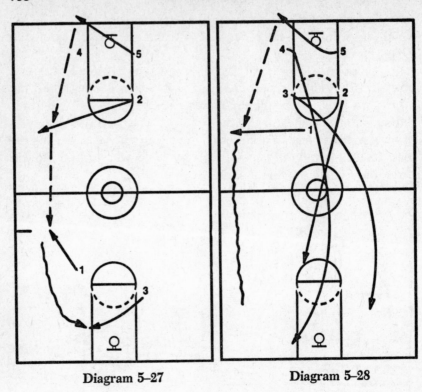

Diagram 5–27   Diagram 5–28

The sideline fast break after a made free-throw is a number eight break. This fast break is illustrated in *Diagram 5–28*. 5 makes the in-bounds pass to 1 who dribbles the ball the length of the floor up the sideline. 2 fills the middle lane and 3 takes the left outside lane. 4 is to move quickly from the back court to the ball side low post area in the front court. 1 looks to pass to 4 down low or swing the ball back to 2 who reverses the ball to 3 for a jumper or a pass, *Diagram 5–29*. If 3 does not have the jump shot he looks for 5 who has been a safety coming down the lane.

In using the numbered break system the coach will, of course, realize that sometimes he will not have the personnel to run some of these breaks and will not use those numbered breaks. Also, the numbers can be changed any year to keep opponents from learning

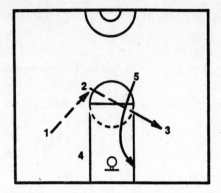

Diagram 5–29

the type of fast break the team is planning to run before the break even materializes.

THE POST-UP MANEUVER

The post-up maneuver is a very effective fast break technique following a missed free-throw which can reap many benefits. The free-throw alignment is shown in *Diagram 5–30*. Notice we have changed the 2 and 3 man's position from our usual alignment.

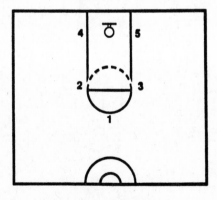

Diagram 5–30

In the post-up maneuver, signalled by yelling *Post*, the number 5 man is the in-bounds passer. 2 is the in-bounds receiver and, once he catches it, has the responsibility of passing the ball to 1 who is using a diagonal cut to the ball from his initial alignment. 2 then fills the right outside lane and 1 fills the middle lane with the basketball. 3 has the task of filling the left outside lane. 4 has the right trailer lane and 5 the left. This sequence is shown in *Diagram 5–31*. Of course the team should always look for the layup from 1, 2, or 3, but a lot of times it is not there and this is when to utilize the so called post-up maneuver. Its beginning is shown in *Diagram 5–32*. In this maneuver, 3 takes his man to the goal and tries to get him on his back, receives the pass from 1, and makes the power play. If 3 is not open for the pass the post-up maneuver keeps going. *Diagram 5–33* illustrates. Now 1 passes the ball to 2 and

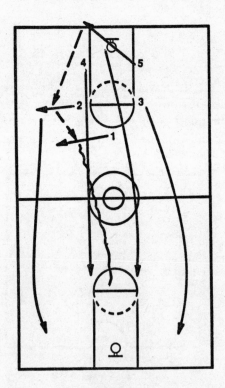

Diagram 5–31

slides down the lane trying to get the man in this area on his back so he can receive the pass from 2. If this is not open the maneuver continues as in *Diagram 5-34* by 2 swinging the ball to 4 out front. At this time 3 has popped out to the left wing area and 5 has posted down low on 3's side. When 3 receives the ball he looks for 5 who is keeping his defensive man on his back away from the ball so he can receive the pass from 3.

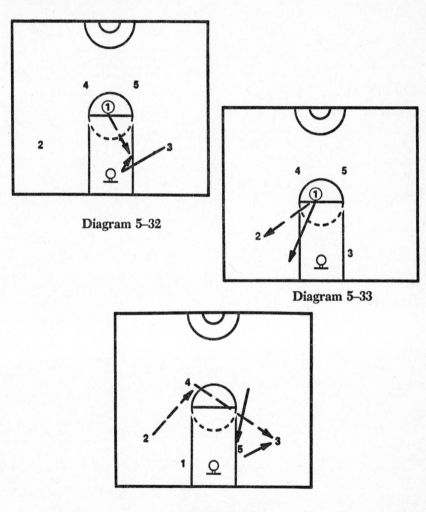

Diagram 5-32

Diagram 5-33

Diagram 5-34

6

FAST BREAKING AGAINST
THE VARIOUS ZONE DEFENSES

Zone defenses have been used in basketball for many years. Zone defenses were used by most teams in the 1950's; then there was a trend away from them in the 60's, and now they have again become quite prevalent. Probably the man to man defenses are most often more effective, but there is also a place for zone defenses, and a coach should always have a good zone his team can use defensively.

Zone defenses seem to be used more at the high school level than at any other level. Even so, a coach at any level must understand zone defenses whether he uses them or not so that he can prepare his team to attack these defenses. It is imperative when teaching offense that a team know the characteristics of any type zone. This is true for any offense whether it be the fast break, set patterns, free lance, delay game, or any press offense.

2–3 ZONE

The 2-3 zone defense is one of the most popular defenses in that it provides good rebounding. In teaching the fast break system to a team, it is necessary to understand the 2-3 zone, how it plays, and how a team should attack it. A primary goal is to get the ball down the floor so quickly the defense does not have time to set up. Hopefully, a team can score before the 2-3 zone has time to set. However, there will be times the fast break will face the 2-3 zone setup.

Diagram 6–1 shows the 2-3 zone alignment when the ball is out front. X1 and X2 protect the ball; X3 is responsible for the high post area; and X4 and X5 have the respective low post areas on their side.

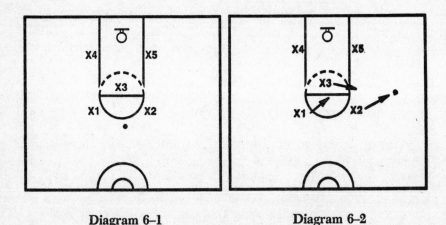

Diagram 6–1   Diagram 6–2

Diagram 6–2 illustrates the basic shifts of the 2-3 zone when the ball is at the right wing. X2 guards the ball; X3 protects the high post; X5 has the ball side low post; X4 defends the low post opposite the ball; and X1 sags to the middle.

In *Diagram 6–3* when the ball is at the left wing, the shifts are the same but responsibilities are different. X1 now has the ball; X3 keeps protecting the high post; X4 now defends the ball side low post while X5 defends the low post away from the ball; and X2 sags to the middle.

Diagram 6–4 shows the slides when the ball is in the right corner. X5 protects the ball; X3 slides to the low post on ball side; X2 protects the high post area; X4 has the offside low post area; and X1 sags to the middle.

These shifts are shown with the ball at the left corner area in Diagram 6–5. Responsibilities are a little different in that X4 defends the ball; X1 protects the high post area; X5 keeps the ball from coming into the offside low post; and X2 sags to the middle. X3 has the same responsibility of defending the ball-side low post.

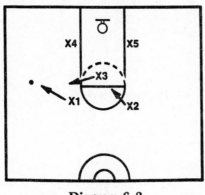

Diagram 6–3

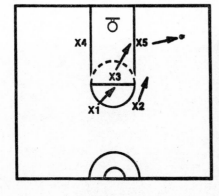

Diagram 6–4

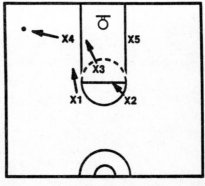

Diagram 6–5

Diagrams 6–6 and *6–7* show a different shift from the basic 2-3 zone when the ball is at the wing areas. Many teams use this type shift as opposed to the shifts illustrated in *Diagrams 6–2* and *6–3*. The change in assignments occurs on the right wing with X2, X3, and X5. X5 is responsible for defending the ball, X3 the low post, and X2 the high post. On the left side X4 takes the ball, X3 the low post, and X1 the high post. X2 and X5 stay the same.

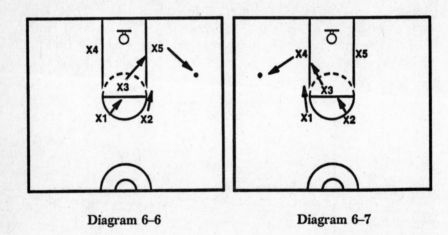

Diagram 6–6   Diagram 6–7

A coach must know, whether it be through scouting reports or studying the zone during the game, which of these techniques the opponent is going to use when guarding the wing so that he can emphasize roles to players filling the outside lanes. If the 2-3 zone is utilizing the slides illustrated in *Diagrams 6–2* and *6–3* and the men in the outside lane do not get a layup from the initial wave cut, *Diagram 6–8*, the outside lanes should break to the deepest wing area possible to make the guard covering the ball, X2 in *Diagram 6–2* and X1 in *Diagram 6–3*, go one or two steps further to get to the ball. What the fast breaking team is trying to do is make the guard have to come longer to defend the ball. This should enable the offense to get more jumpers at the wing area against this zone. *Diagram 6–9* illustrates an outside lane setting up deeper than the usual wing area and shows that the defensive guard must come further than normal. This move can usually make the guard come an extra one to two feet and the extra distance allows the offense more wing shots.

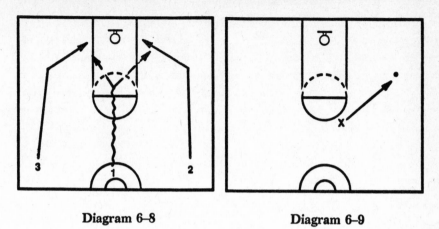

Diagram 6–8   Diagram 6–9

The reasoning behind this technique is also something to keep in mind when the back men in the 2-3 zone cover the wings, *Diagrams 6–6* and *6–7*. When the back men are covering the wings and the outside lanes are not going to get the layup, the outside lanes can break to a high wing area, *Diagram 6–10*. This makes the back men take a step or two higher than usual giving us extra time and usually more shots from the wing area.

Diagram 6–10

When using the two guard break system, described in Chapter 3, against the 2-3 zone with the opponent's guards covering the wings, the break will look as shown in *Diagram 6–11* with 4 rebounding the ball as an example. Notice the outside lanes have

moved to the deep wing area. Once the ball is passed to the wing, 3
in this case, *Diagram 6–12*, he will look for a quick jumper or to
pass to 5 low. 4 slides to the opposite low post on the pass and 1 is
at the outside lane opposite 3. 2, upon the pass to 3, slides a step or
two to ball side. This is illustrated in *Diagram 6–12*. If the offense
does not have a shot off this, the team needs to attack the weaknesses of the zone with the fast break continuing. The weaknesses of
the 2-3 zone guards are at the wing areas and high post areas;
therefore, there should be movement of the ball and movement of
men in these areas.

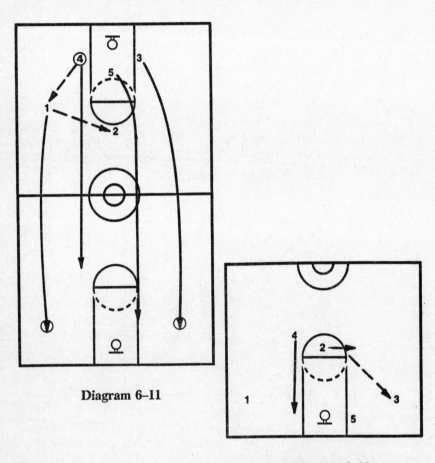

Diagram 6–11

Diagram 6–12

The offensive team continues its fast break against the 2-3 zone, using *Diagram 6–13* as an illustration, by flashing 4 to the ball-side high post. Hopefully, there will be a pass to him for a shot or pass. If not, the team can look to move the ball to the other side to 1 at a deep wing area for an open jumper.

Diagram 6–14 illustrates the two guard break against the 2-3 zone that defenses the ball at the wing with their back men, *Diagrams 6–6* and *6–7*, with 4 rebounding. The break is the same, but the outside lanes break to a high wing area. The break remains the same as described in *Diagrams 6–12* and *6–13*.

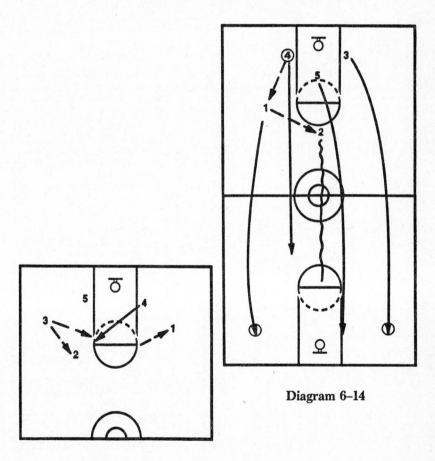

Diagram 6–14

Diagram 6–13

If a team uses the controlled break as described in Chapter 3, the techniques against the 2-3 zone will remain the same as described in this chapter.

Diagram 6-15 shows an example of the controlled break going to the deep wing area and *Diagram 6-16* shows the controlled break going to the high wing areas. The sideline break is also the same as described in Chapter 3 except the ball is dribbled down the side instead of the middle to the deep wing or high wing areas.

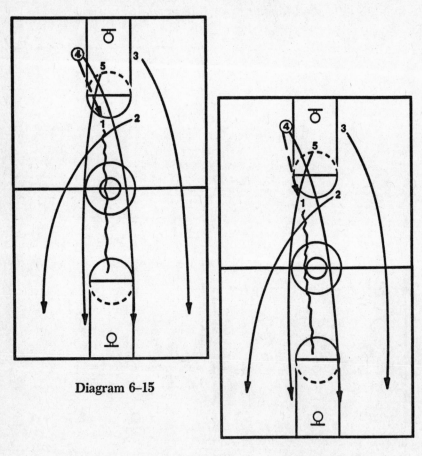

Diagram 6-15

Diagram 6-16

THE 1-2-2 ZONE

The 1-2-2 zone is a spread type zone. It is a very effective zone in defensing the perimeter, and its weaknesses are in the lane area, *Diagram 6–17*, and as with other zones it is vulnerable to quick and sharp movement of the ball and movement of men. Penetration of the ball is also effective against this zone. To better understand this zone for a more effective fast break, the shifts of the zone are shown in *Diagrams 6–18* through *6–23*.

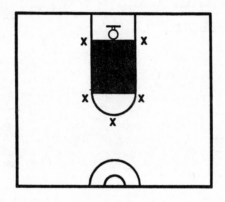

Diagram 6–17

Diagrams 6–18 and *6–19* show the zone setup when the ball is out front. X1 is protecting the ball, X2 protects the middle in *Diagram 6–18* when the ball is out front and to the right, and X3 protects the middle when the ball is out front and to the left. Everybody else protects his area as shown.

Diagram 6–20 illustrates the slides of the 1-2-2 zone when the ball is at the left wing area. X2 defends the ball; X4 and X5 protect the low posts in their respective areas; X1 defends the high post area; and X3 sags to the middle.

In *Diagram 6–21*, X3 defends the ball when it is at the right wing area. X4 and X5 maintain defense at their low post areas; X1 has the high post area; and X2 sags to the middle.

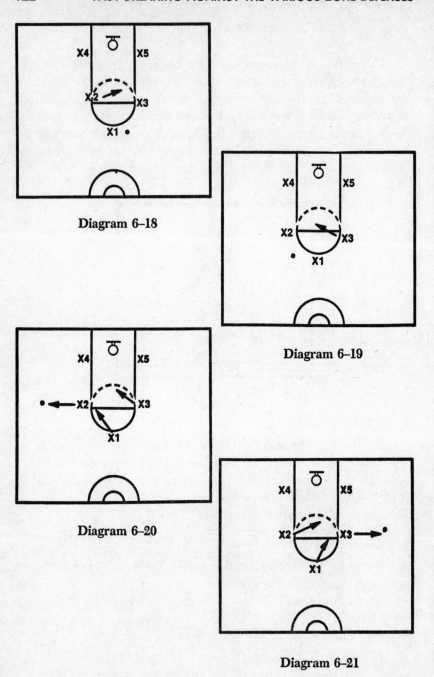

Diagram 6–18

Diagram 6–19

Diagram 6–20

Diagram 6–21

Diagram 6–22 shows the responsibilities of the 1-2-2 zone when the ball is in the left corner. X4 must defend the ball; X5 slides to the ball-side low post; X2 has the high post; X1 clogs the middle; and X3 slides down to the low post away from the ball.

Diagram 6–23 illustrates the right corner slides from the 1-2-2 zone. X5 defends the ball; X4 protects the ball-side low post area; X3 defends the high post area; X1 clogs the middle; and X2 slides down to contain the low post area opposite X4.

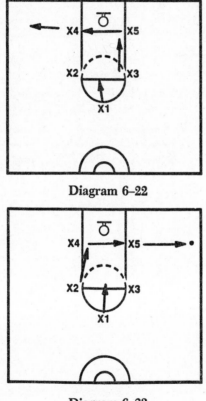

Diagram 6–22

Diagram 6–23

When breaking against this zone, the initial goal is to get the ball down the floor and try to score a layup off the initial wave. If this goal is not achieved, the fast breaking team will move the ball and men into the weaknesses of this zone. When the fast break is not going to get the layup, the men in the outside lanes break all the way to the corners, *Diagram 6–24*, in order to attack the lane area where this zone is weak. *Diagram 6–25* shows an example with offensive men in the lane area. The back two men of the 1-2-2 zone, X4 and X5, are involved in the defense. When X5 slides to defend the ball X4 has the responsibility of guarding the ball-side low post. If the post man executes a good job of posting, he should be able to keep X4 behind him at all times and be able to receive this pass at will. This is the main reason to break to the corners from the outside lane so that the offense will be in a position to attack the zone's weakness, the lane area, by hitting the low post man with a pass. The lane area is also weak in the high post area. In *Diagrams 6–22* and *6–23* one of the opponent's guards will be defending any of the post players that flash into this area. The post player's height and strength should allow him to receive the pass over a guard.

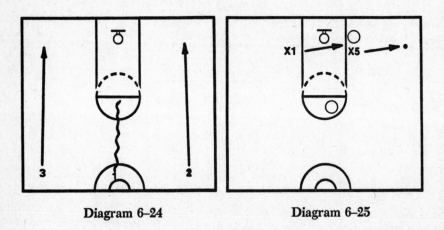

Diagram 6–24   Diagram 6–25

Diagram 6–26 gives an example of the two guard break against the 1-2-2 zone defense with 5 rebounding from the defense. 2 has the ball in the middle lane; 1 has filled the right outside lane; 2 the left outside lane; 4 is first to the low post block; and 5 is a safety and fills the opposite low post on the first pass in the front

court. The offense is now in the positions shown in *Diagram 6–27*
with 1 having received the first pass from 2. 1 looks to the weakness
of the zone where 4 is located and tries to hit him with a pass. If 4 is
not open he looks to pass to 5 breaking into the high post area
against their guard for a shot. This sequence is seen in *Diagram
6–28*. If there is nothing open to either 4 or 5 the ball is swung back
to 2 who passes to 3 in the left corner. 3 now looks for 4 sliding back
across the lane low and 5 flashing across to the ball side high post
area. This is illustrated in *Diagram 6–29*.

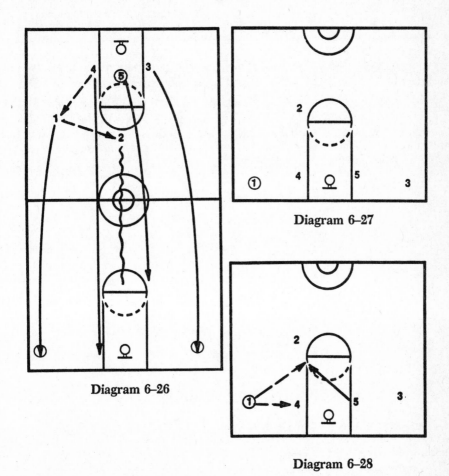

Diagram 6–26

Diagram 6–27

Diagram 6–28

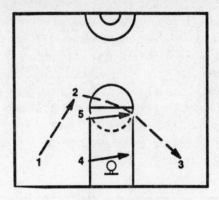

Diagram 6–29

Sometimes effective against a 1-2-2 zone is an X maneuver with the post men when the ball is swung from one side of the court to the other side. This is shown in *Diagram 6–30*. 4 flashes to the high post and 5 slides to the low post on the swing of the ball. This maneuver is another attempt to attack the weaknesses of the 1-2-2 zone.

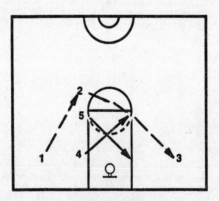

Diagram 6–30

The controlled break techniques are run the same as the two guard break and is shown in *Diagram 6–31* with 5 rebounding the ball and each lane being filled properly. *Diagram 6–32* illustrates the swing of the ball from one side of the floor to the other, using 2's side to start the swing of the ball on. Notice 4 flashed to the high post on 2's side.

Since the sideline break, as described in Chapter 3, is already effective against a 1-2-2 zone formation, there is little need for variation. The only difference is that the dribbler has the responsibility of dribbling the ball to the corner, but the techniques for attacking the lane area remain the same.

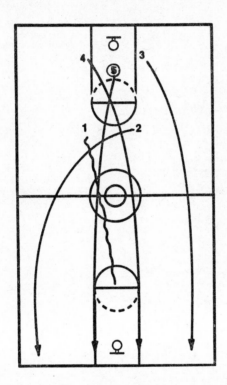

Diagram 6–31

THE 1-3-1 ZONE

One of the more widely used zones across the country is the 1-3-1 zone defense. Some of the finer college teams across the nation, such as Kentucky, have executed this defense to perfection helping to prove themselves worthy of national acclaim. Many state champions at the high school level have used the 1-3-1 zone to help them reach their pinnacle.

The slides and coverages of this zone are shown in *Diagrams 6–32 through 6–38.*

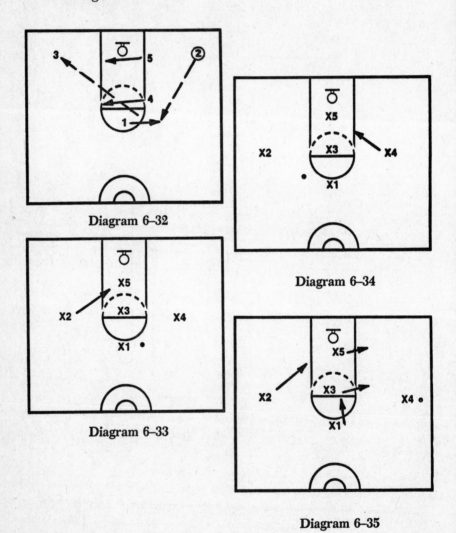

Diagram 6–32

Diagram 6–33

Diagram 6–34

Diagram 6–35

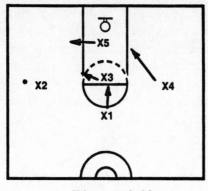

Diagram 6–36

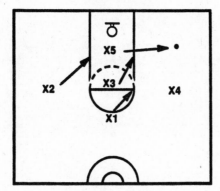

Diagram 6–37

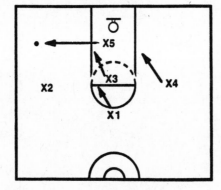

Diagram 6–38

Diagrams 6–33 and *6–34* show the 1-3-1 zone alignment with X1 taking the ball out front and the other defensive men covering their respective areas shown in the alignment. One additional note to remember is that the offside wing, either X2 or X4, is responsible for cross-court passes from out front made to the opposite corner, *Diagrams 6–39* and *6–40*, and X5 has the ball-side low post when the ball is out front.

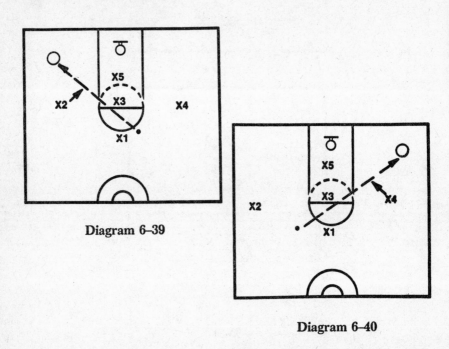

Diagram 6–39

Diagram 6–40

The slides of the 1-3-1 zone defense when the ball is at the right wing area are shown in *Diagram 6–35*. X4 defends the ball; X5 covers the ball side low post; X3 takes the high post area; X1 sags to the middle; and X2 is responsible for the offside rebound on shots or any cross-court passes.

Diagram 6–36 illustrates the movement of men in the 1-3-1 zone from the left wing area. X2 defends the ball; X5 contains the ball side low post area; X3 protects the high post area; X1 sags to the middle; and X4 now has the offside area.

Diagram 6–37 shows the slides when the ball is in the right corner. X5 slides out from the basket area and defends the ball; X3 drops down low to protect the ball side post; X2 has the responsibility of guarding the offside area; X1 defends the high post area; and X4 plays the passing lane for the pass from the corner to the pass out front.

In *Diagram 6–38* X5 is defending the ball; X3 has the ball side low post; X2 plays in the passing lane out front; X4 protects the offside area; and X1 defends the high post area.

The strengths of this zone are in the wing areas, and weaknesses tend to be at the corner area and out front as there is usually one man assigned to cover these areas. Again, as in all zones, passing of the ball, penetration, and movement of men are important points to emphasize when fast breaking this particular type of zone.

In the two guard break, if there is no layup from the initial wave or first three lanes, the men in the outside lanes break to the corners to attack the weaknesses of the zone. The lane filling is the same as the example in *Diagrams 6–26* and *6–27* against the 1-2-2 zone. The two guard break is the same as against the 1-2-2 zone except when the ball is swung from one side of the floor to the other. This is illustrated in *Diagram 6–41*. When the ball is swung from 1 to 2, 3 will break to the front of the zone where there is a weakness in that only one man is guarding the front area. He is looking for the jumper in this area. Against the 1-3-1 zone we also emphasize no flashes to the high post area when the ball is in the corner until the ball has been swung. We feel the 1-3-1 zone is relatively strong at the high post area when the ball is in the corner. Once the ball has been swung to 3, the fast break continues attacking weaknesses if 3 does not take a shot. *Diagram 6–42* illustrates the movement. 1 slides across the baseline to 3's side looking for a shot and 4 flashes to the high post looking for a shot or good pass to make.

This same action is done when the ball is swung from 3's side after the initial pass from 2 and is shown in *Diagram 6–43*. This fast break action against the 1-3-1 zone will produce baskets in that it attacks the weaknesses of the 1-3-1 zone.

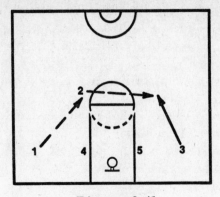

Diagram 6–41

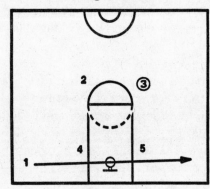

Diagram 6–42

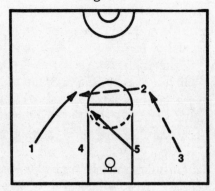

Diagram 6–43

The controlled break and the sideline break fill the same lanes as described in Chapter 3, and once the lanes are filled the players execute the same movements described in *Diagrams 6–41* through *6–43* when fast breaking against the 1-3-1 zone.

Once the ball has been swung over against any zone and a shot does not develop from the break, the offense should set up a pattern and run a particular offense against a particular defense.

7

FAST BREAKING FROM THE
VARIOUS PRESSING DEFENSES

Many teams develop the fast break to score after situations that occur in the front court from around the basket such as a missed or made field goal or a missed or made free-throw. Pressing defenses allows another dimension to the fast break. This dimension is scoring with a fast break that comes from a steal in the pressing defenses.

During one season, approximately 30 percent of our points came from fast break situations that occurred off steals in our pressing defenses. There were times when over half of our points in a game came from scoring on the fast break after a steal.

When a team can take advantage of mistakes made by the opponent the opponent becomes frustrated. Frustration always comes to the opponent when a team makes a steal off the press and turns this fast break situation into a score.

When a team steals the ball off a press, the coach should emphasize scoring within 2 seconds if the ball is stolen in the back court, 3 seconds if it has been taken at the mid-court area, and 4 seconds if it is stolen in the front court. This will encourage the players to take advantage of the mistake quickly and frustrate the opponent.

THE 1-2-1-1 ZONE PRESS

The 1-2-1-1 zone press is one of a variety of presses used to try to get an intercepted pass. The steal can turn the opponent's pass into a fast break situation and a score.

Most teams use the 1-2-1-1 zone press after a successful field goal or free-throw. It can force the opponent to hurry and make him play the fast game. Teams that try to play a control or semi-control game against a team that presses in the back court will find it very difficult to do.

Fast breaking off the full court zone press is the quickest method of getting the ball on defense and putting it into the basket. If a team starts a game in a press, steals the ball a few times, and turns the steals into scores they have complete control of the game. Many teams have even been behind several points in games and they have utilized the 1-2-1-1 full court zone press and have won due to their ability to get the ball and score quickly.

Above all, when a team starts stealing the ball and scoring off this press, they become aggressive, and this is one of the most important characteristics of playing fast break basketball.

The 1-2-1-1 full court zone press is one of my favorite zone presses and is covered thoroughly in my book entitled *Zone Press Variations for Winning Basketball*. Its alignment is shown in *Diagram 7–1*. The basic trap areas are illustrated in the shaded circles in *Diagram 7–2*.

Diagram 7–3 shows the basic coverages of the 1-2-1-1 press when the ball is trapped in the left corner. X1 and X2 double team the ball. X3 covers the lateral and back pass area. X4 is responsible for steals in the sideline area, and X5 has the middle area and is also the safety man.

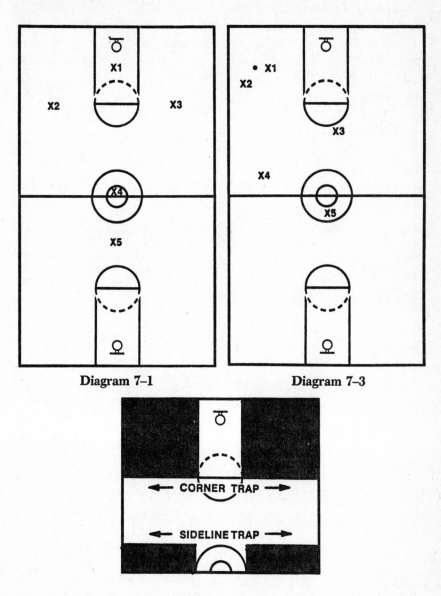

Diagram 7–1   Diagram 7–3

Diagram 7–2

Diagram 7–4 illustrates the initial trap of the ball in the right corner area. X1 and X3 trap the ball. X2 tries to steal the lateral or back pass. X4 covers the sideline area, and X5 has the middle and safety area.

The left sideline trap basic coverages are shown in *Diagram 7–5*. X1 and X4 double team the ball. X2 has the side pass coverage. X3 has the middle area in the front court, and X5 covers the sideline.

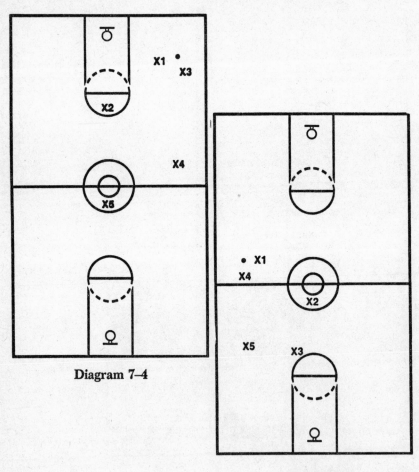

Diagram 7–4

Diagram 7–5

The basic responsibilities of the right sideline trap are illustrated in *Diagram 7-6*. X1 and X4 trap the ball. X3 is responsible for the lateral pass area, X2 the middle area in the front court, and X5 the sideline.

Upon stealing the ball from the corner traps in the 1-2-1-1 full court zone press, the team should score within 2 to 3 seconds. When a steal is made from the corner trap, players have certain responsibilities.

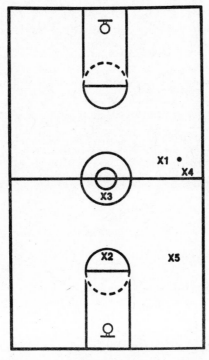

Diagram 7-6

Diagram 7-7 illustrates each man's responsibility when the ball is stolen by X3 from the left corner trap. Most often X3 will get an unmolested layup because of the area in which his steals come from. Most teams will have a receiver in the four areas shown in

Diagram 7–8. These areas are the lateral pass area, 1; the middle area, 2; the sideline area, 3; and the deep pass area, 4. When the steal comes in the lateral pass area, the fast break situation should be an unmolested one. If it is not unmolested, a team should have at least a two on one fast break situation. When X3 steals the ball he goes directly to the hole. X1 goes to the opposite block of the dribbler. If X3 is picked up by a defensive man, he looks to pass to X1 in his area. This will occur almost 50 percent of the time in a situation where there is a defensive man contesting the ball. X2's job is to go to the middle lane area, be a receiver for a shot or pass and follow up for any rebounds. Because of the nature of the steal by X3, X4 and X5 stay behind the ball and act as safeties. This is because so many of the opponent's men will be in the mid-court and back court areas when the lateral pass is stolen.

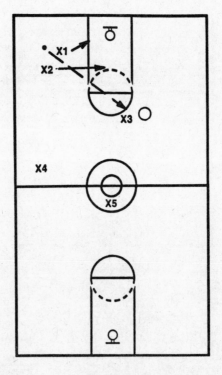

Diagram 7–7

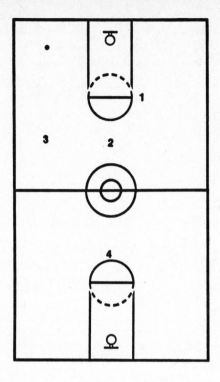

Diagram 7–8

The same techniques are used when the lateral pass is stolen by X2 from the right corner trap, *Diagram 7–9*. X2 steals the ball and goes directly to the basket. X1 goes to the opposite low post area looking for a pass, shot, or rebound. X3 is responsible for going to the middle of the lane for a pass, shot or rebound. X4 and X5 are the safeties.

Diagram 7–10 shows the fast break after a steal from the left corner trap by X5. When X5 steals the ball he is in the middle lane of the fast break. He takes the ball down this lane directly to the basket until he is contested by the defense. X3 flares from his defensive position and has the right outside lane. X2 takes the left outside lane from his trap technique. X1 goes to either low post block. He goes to the block that he feels is most vulnerable for a score. X4 is a safety and stays behind the ball at all times in this fast break. X5 has the options of shooting or passing to X1, X2, or X3 for a score. As in all our fast break situations after a steal, the team must set their regular half court offense if a score does not come off this initial wave by X5, X1, X2, and X3. This is done because some players will be in unfamiliar spots offensively if the initial wave does not score and they should not run free-lance plays from these areas.

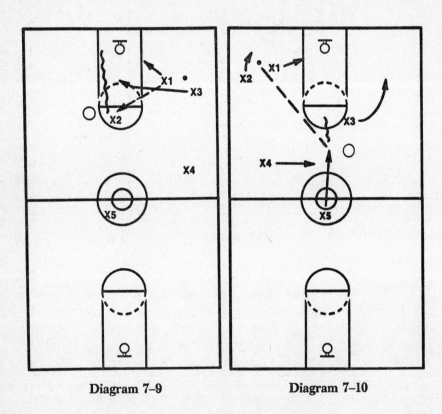

Diagram 7–9   Diagram 7–10

The right corner trap steal by X5 is illustrated in *Diagram 7–11*. X5 steals the ball and fills the middle lane with the ball. X2 has the left outside lane while X3 takes the right outside lane. X1 goes to the low post area and X4 is the safety.

The lane coverages are almost the same when X4 steals the ball from the left corner trap at the sideline area as when X5 steals the ball in the middle area. This is depicted in *Diagram 7–12*. X4 steals the ball, fills the middle lane, and goes directly to the basket until picked up by the defense. X1 fills the low post area he feels has the best scoring opportunity. X2 fills the left outside lane and X3 has the right outside lane. X5 now becomes the safety man staying behind the ball in case the defense gets it. X4 can shoot or pass to X1, X2, or X3 for a scoring opportunity.

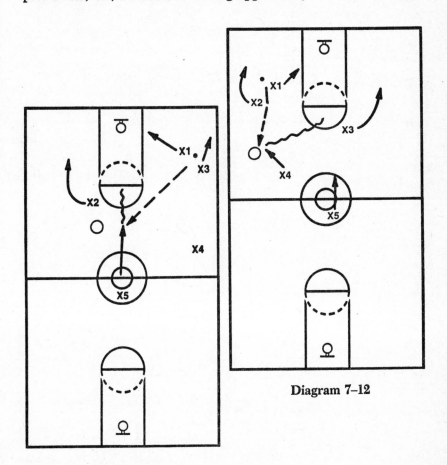

Diagram 7–12

Diagram 7–11

The sideline steal from the right corner trap is illustrated in *Diagram 7–13*. X4 fills the middle lane with the ball. X1 fills the low post area while X2 and X3 fill the left and right outside lanes respectively. X5 remains the safety. Again, X4 looks to score or pass to X1, X2, or X3 for a possible score.

If X1 were to steal the ball in some way from the corner trap, left corner trap for example in *Diagram 7–14*, he dribbles the ball directly to the basket to shoot or pass to X3 who goes to the opposite low post or X2 who goes to the middle lane area. X4 and X5 stay back as safeties. X1 does the same thing on steals from the right corner trap, *Diagram 7–15*, looking for a shot or pass to X2 or X3.

Everything remains the same in the fast break situation when X2 or X3 steals the ball from the trap as when X1 steals the ball.

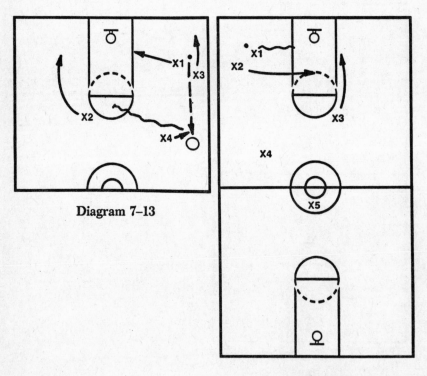

Diagram 7–13

Diagram 7–14

The only difference is that X1 swaps assignments with the stealer, X2 or X3. The steal by X2 or X3 from the left or right corner traps and the fast break from these situations are shown in *Diagrams 7–16* and *7–17*.

The steal and fast break rules from the sideline traps in the 1-2-1-1 zone press are the same as a steal and fast break from the three quarter court press which is covered in this chapter.

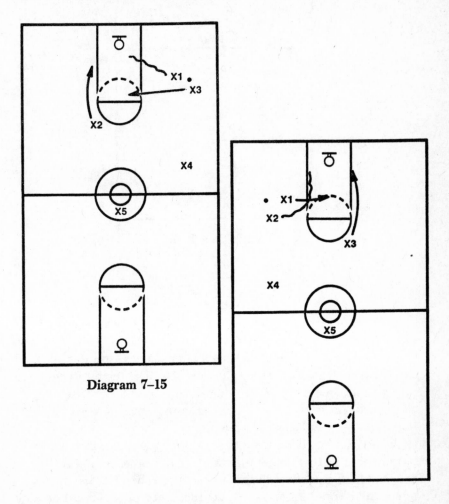

Diagram 7–15

Diagram 7–16

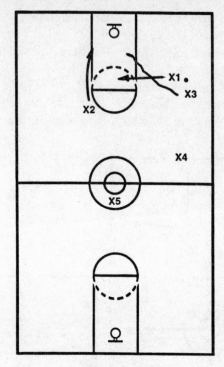

Diagram 7–17

THE 2-2-1 ZONE PRESS

The 2-2-1 three quarter court zone press is a very good, conservative press in that the gambles taken are not as great as in the full court press. It is basically used after a successful field goal or free-throw. Many coaches employ it when their teams do not have much depth. A team with no depth can not afford to use the full court zone press the whole game because they may get into too much foul trouble by being aggressive all over the floor. This press allows a team to take advantage of the opponent that has poor passing ability. It is hoped that the ball will be trapped every time near the hash mark area in the back court. When this happens, the opponent has one alternative and that is to pass. Therefore, the team using this defense is looking to steal the bad pass, turn it into a fast break and score.

The floor alignment of the 2-2-1 three quarter court zone press is shown in *Diagram 7–18*. The shaded areas in *Diagram 7–19* show the basic trap areas for this press.

Diagram 7–20 illustrates the basic defensive coverage of the 2-2-1 three quarter court press when the ball is trapped on the left side. X1 and X3 double team the man with the ball. X2 covers the area near the half court circle. X5 has the responsibility of stopping all passes to the sideline area. X4 is responsible for passes into the middle area in front court.

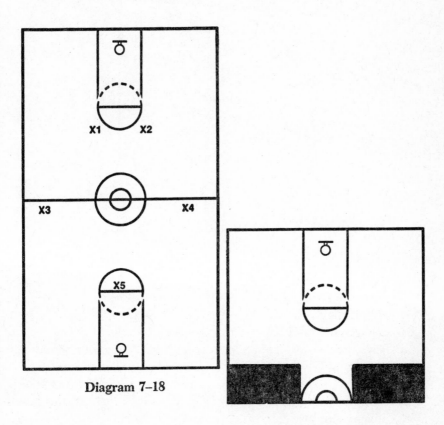

Diagram 7–18

Diagram 7–19

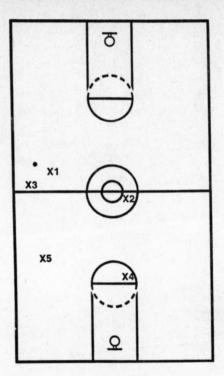

Diagram 7–20

The basic defensive coverages when the ball is trapped at the right sideline are shown in *Diagram 7–21*. X2 and X4 trap the ball. X1 covers the area near the time line; X3 has the middle area; and X5 stops the sideline passes.

When the ball is stolen from the mid-court area off this press there should be a score in 3 seconds. This usually occurs off steals from the trappers and the player covering the area near the time line. Players who steal the ball in the sideline and middle areas of this press try to help get a fast break score within four seconds.

Diagram 7–22 illustrates the fast break responsibilities of each man when the ball is stolen by X2 from the trap at the left sideline. These responsibilities also exist when this sideline trap is used in the full court zone press. In most cases X2 will get an easy layup because he usually gets way out in front of the defense when steal-

ing the ball. If X2 is contested by the defense which is usually a two
on one fast break situation, he takes the ball straight to the hole and, if
he does not have a layup, looks to the opposite block for X1 who has
filled this area. X3 fills the middle lane to be a receiver for a shot or
pass and follow up on any missed shots by X1 or X2. X4 and X5 stay
behind the ball and are safeties in case the opponent gets the ball
back.

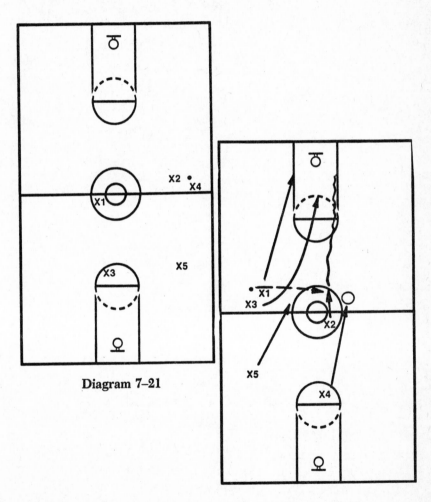

Diagram 7–21

Diagram 7–22

This steal from the right sideline trap is shown in *Diagram 7–23*. X1 dribbles the ball directly to the basket and X2 goes to the opposite block. X4 fills the middle lane while X3 and X5 act as the safeties.

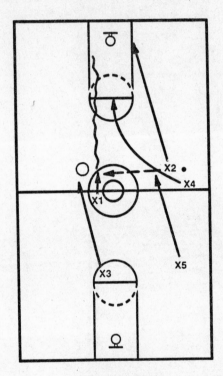

Diagram 7–23

Diagram 7–24 illustrates the fast break responsibilities when the ball is stolen from the left sideline trap by X4 at the middle area in the front court. X4, upon stealing the ball, fills the middle lane and, if he gets ahead of the defense, goes for the layup. If the defense stops him, he looks to pass for a score to X2, who has filled the right outside lane; X1 in the left outside lane; or X3 in the low post area. X3 in the 2-2-1 three quarter court trap is usually a bigger player than X1; therefore, we want him at the post area instead of X1.

However, if a team plays this press with big men on the front line in a trap, they should use X1 as the player who posts up when the ball is stolen by X4 from the left sideline trap. X5 is the safety man in this fast break situation.

The steal and fast break from the middle area off the right sideline trap is shown in *Diagram 7–25*. X3 steals the ball and fills the middle lane; X1 takes the left outside lane; X2, the right outside lane; X4 goes to the low post area on either side of the floor; and X5 is the safety.

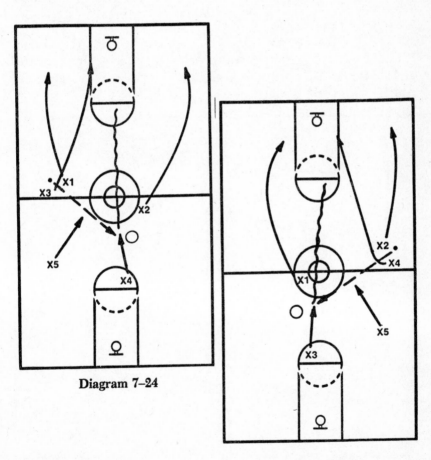

Diagram 7–24

Diagram 7–25

As mentioned earlier, when steals from the press and the fast break following produce no score the half court offense should be set up.

The fast break responsibilities after a steal from the left sideline trap by X5 in the 2-2-1 three quarter court press are shown in *Diagram 7–26*. X5 takes the pass and fills the middle lane with the ball. X2 has the responsibility of filling the right outside lane while X1 has the left outside lane. X3 goes to the low post area of his choice. X4 has safety responsibility. X5 looks to score or pass to X1, X2, or X3 for a scoring opportunity.

These responsibilities when X5 steals the ball from the right sideline trap are shown in *Diagram 7–27*. Again, X5 fills the middle lane with the ball. X1 is responsible for filling the left outside lane and X2 has the right outside lane. X4 posts up low in this situation and X3 is the safety man.

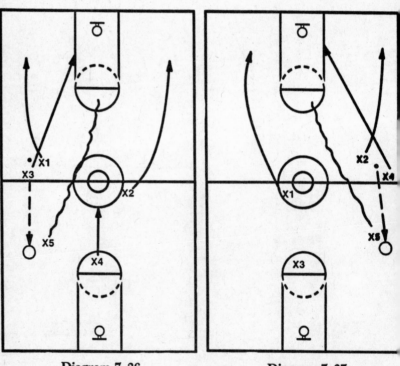

Diagram 7–26   Diagram 7–27

If X1 were to steal the ball out of the left sideline trap, *Diagram 7–28*, he should be in front of the defense. X1 should dribble the ball to the basket and look to score or pass for a score to X2 who goes to the block opposite the dribbler or X3 in the middle lane. X4 and X5 stay behind the ball for safety responsibility.

These same fast break responsibilities are used when X2 steals the ball out of the right sideline trap and are illustrated in *Diagram 7–29*. X3 and X5 are safeties. X2 goes to the basket down the right side with the basketball; X1 goes to the block opposite X2; and X4 fills the middle lane.

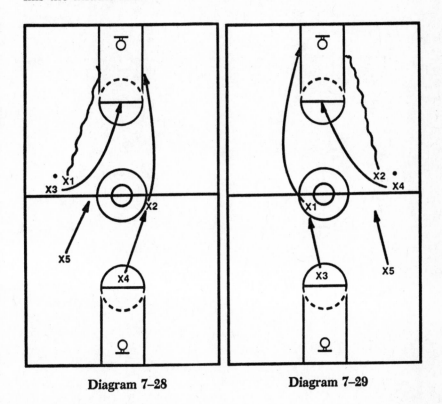

Diagram 7–28   Diagram 7–29

The fast break remains the same when X3 steals the ball from the left sideline trap as when X1 steals it, *Diagram 7–30*, except X1 and X3 swap responsibilities. From the right sideline trap, the fast break is also the same when X4 steals the ball as when X2 does, *Diagram 7–31*, except X2 and X4 swap assignments.

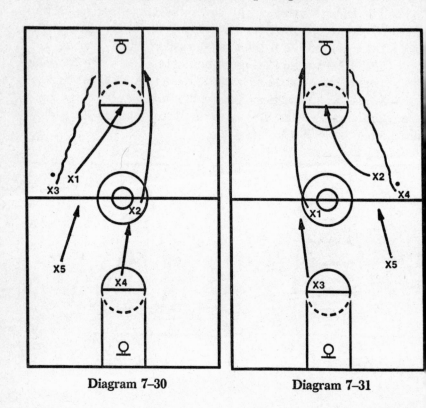

Diagram 7–30   Diagram 7–31

THE 1-3-1 TRAP

The 1-3-1 half court trap can be set up and used whether a field goal is made or missed offensively. There are four basic trap areas in this press and they are shown with shaded areas in *Diagram 7–32*. In *Diagram 7–33*, the initial alignment of this press can be seen.

Diagram 7–34 shows the trap coverages at the left sideline. X1 and X2 double team the ball. X3 covers the middle pass area in the front court; X5 has the sideline pass area; and X4 takes the pass in the cross-court area.

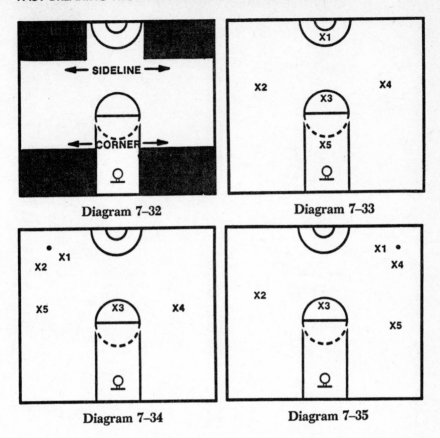

Diagram 7–32

Diagram 7–33

Diagram 7–34

Diagram 7–35

Diagram 7–35 illustrates the right sideline trap coverages. X1 and X4 trap the ball. X5 has sideline responsibility; X3 middle area responsibility; and X2 cross-court responsibility.

The defensive coverages for the left corner trap in the 1-3-1 half court trap are shown in *Diagram 7–36*. X2 and X5 double team the ball in the left corner area. X1 keeps the ball from coming back out front. X3 stops the ball from coming to the low post area while X4 is responsible for stopping the pass into the high post area.

The initial defensive trap from the right corner is shown in *Diagram 7–37*. X4 and X5 trap the ball. X1 stops the ball from coming back out front. X3 keeps the ball out of the low post area. X2 does not let the ball come into the high post area.

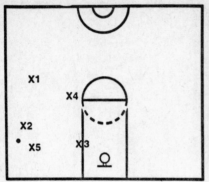

Diagram 7–36   Diagram 7–37

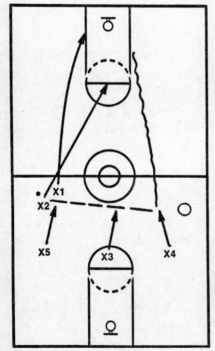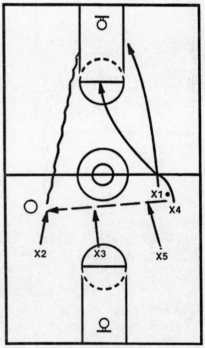

Diagram 7–38   Diagram 7–39

When the ball is stolen by X4 from the left sideline trap of the 1-3-1 press, the fast break responsibilities exist as shown in *Diagram 7–38*. X4 steals the ball and looks to score a layup. If the layup is not there, he looks to pass to X1 at the opposite block or X2 in the middle lane area for a scoring opportunity. X3 and X5 have safety responsibility.

Diagram 7–39 shows the cross-court steal by X2 from the right sideline trap. X2 looks to score or pass to X1 at the opposite block or X 4 in the middle lane area for a score. X3 and X5 are safeties.

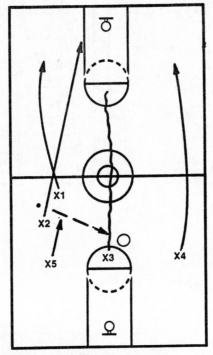

Diagram 7–40

The fast break responsibilities are shown in *Diagram 7–40* when X3 steals the ball in the middle area from the left sideline trap. X3 looks for the layup in the middle lane after the steal. If he is contested by the defense, he looks to pass for a score to X4 in the

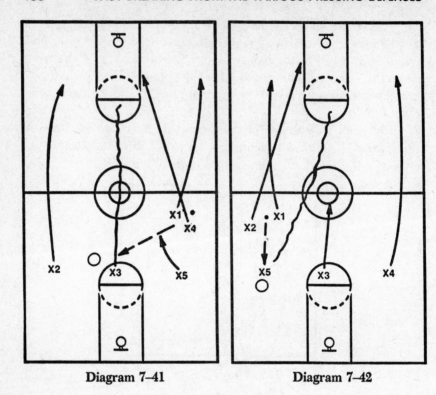

Diagram 7–41   **Diagram 7–42**

right outside lane, X1 in the left outside lane, or X2 in the basket area. X5 will be the safety. The middle area steal by X3 from the right sideline trap and the fast break that follows remain the same. Assignments are a little different and are shown in *Diagram 7–41*.

Diagram 7–42 illustrates the fast break from the steal by X5 off the left sideline trap. X5 looks to score the layup or pass to X4 who fills the right outside lane; to X1 in the left outside lane; or to X2 in the basket area for the scoring opportunity. X3 is the safety man. When X5 steals the ball from the right sideline trap the fast break stays the same, *Diagram 7–43*.

Diagram 7–44 shows the fast break from the 1-3-1 half court trap when X1 steals the ball out of the left sideline trap. X1 dribbles the ball to the basket for a layup. If the defense stops him he should pass to X4 who has filled the low post opposite the ball or to X2 in the middle lane area for a score. X3 and X5 have safety responsibility.

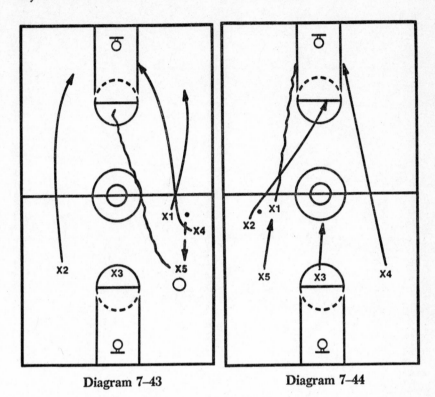

Diagram 7-43   Diagram 7-44

Diagram 7-45 shows the fast break when the steal is made by X1 in the right sideline trap. X1 tries to score or pass for a score to X2 at the opposite low post or to X4 in the middle lane. X3 and X5 are the safeties.

When X2 steals the ball out of the left sideline trap, the fast break is the same as when X1 steals it. X1 and X2 swap assignments when this happens (*Diagram 7-46*). The same technique also occurs when X4 steals the ball out of the right sideline trap as shown in *Diagram 7-47*.

In all corner traps from the 1-3-1 half court trap (*Diagrams 7-36* and *7-37*), the trappers on each side and X3 are in deep areas and far removed from their basket. Therefore, on all steals by trappers and X3, they look to make an outlet pass to X1 who is always out front. His responsibility is to fill the middle lane with the ball. X5 in the 1-3-1 trap is usually a guard and has to be quick

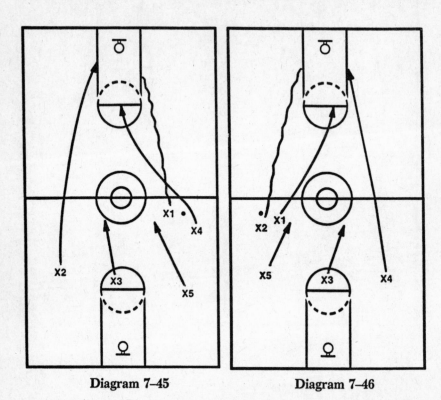

Diagram 7–45   Diagram 7–46

whatever his position because of the area he has to cover defensively. Therefore, he fills the outside lane on the side he corner traps on. The man responsible for stopping the pass to the high post fills the lane opposite the corner trap. Since X3 is the post man, he has the job of sprinting to either low post area when the steal is made posting up for a possible score. These responsibilities always exist when a trapper or X3 steals the ball off the corner trap. An example of this fast break is shown in *Diagram 7–48* with X3 stealing the ball.

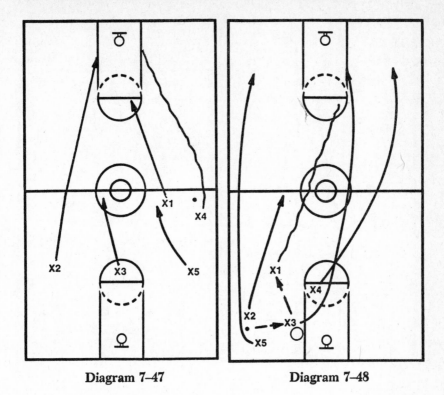

Diagram 7–47   Diagram 7–48

The fast break after a steal by X1 from the left corner trap is shown in *Diagram 7–49*. X1 should get several unmolested layups off this steal or at least face a 2 on 1 situation. If he does not get the layup, he looks to pass to X4 who has the responsibility of going to the low post opposite the ball or to X5 filling the middle lane for any scoring opportunity. X2 and X3 assume safety responsibility.

Diagram 7–50 illustrates the fast break when X1 steals the ball from the right corner trap.

The fast break after a steal by X4 from the left corner trap is shown in *Diagram 7–51*. In this situation, X4 should get a lot of easy layups because he will be able to get out in front of the defense many times. If not, he looks to X1 in the left lane and X5 in the right lane for a scoring opportunity. X2 and X3 assume safety responsibilities.

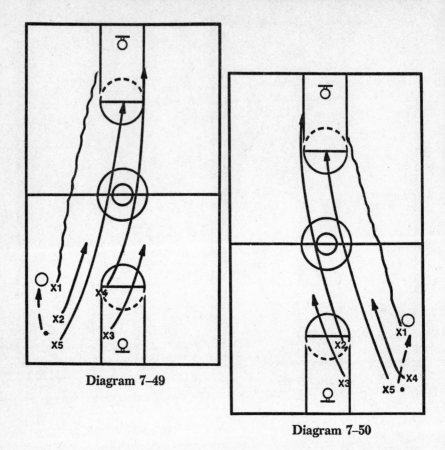

Diagram 7-49

Diagram 7-50

The steal by X2 from the right corner trap and the fast break that occurs are shown in *Diagram 7-52*. X2 steals the ball and dribbles to the basket for a layup or a pass to X1 and X5 in their respective outside lanes. X3 and X4 are safeties.

There are other zone presses at the full court, three quarter court, and half court areas beside the ones used in this chapter. These particular presses have been used to give the coach the methods of fast breaking from each area. The principles and techniques for fast breaking from the other presses are, of course, similar to the ones discussed here, and a coach should be able to adapt this information to his own purposes.

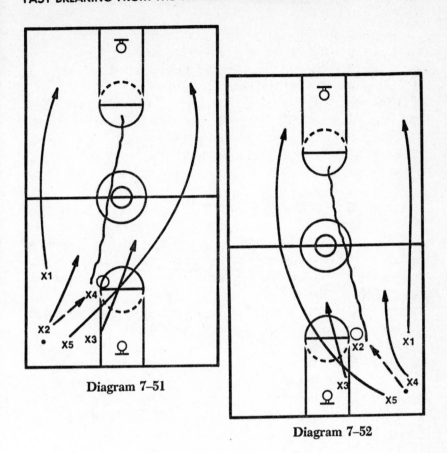

Diagram 7–51

Diagram 7–52

THE MAN TO MAN PRESS

The man to man press has been used successfully by many teams throughout the country at all levels. It requires good quickness and great individual execution. Each defensive man is assigned to a particular offensive man. It is individual talent against individual talent. This is one of the beauties of basketball. If any one of the individuals lets down defensively the entire defense will suffer. Great individual defense by everyone will usually create steal or turnover opportunities that can be turned into fast breaks and easy scores.

A great man to man press can stop the team that has the offensive super stars. If the man to man pressure defense can cause the opponents to turn the ball over before the super stars can shoot, then the defense will more than likely win.

The man to man press, like the zone press, forces the offensive team to attack. They cannot stand still with the basketball. This complements the fast break. The defender can force the opponent to play his type of basketball. Any time the right type of pressure is applied, an offensive team will not be able to sit on the basketball.

The fast break to use when the ball is stolen in the man to man press is determined by the interceptor. Everyone has certain rules to abide by when he intercepts a pass. When utilizing the man to man press the defensive players will be in various spots at various times. Therefore, the team should use rules on the intercepted pass. When a defensive man steals the ball, he has three basic options. One option is to feed anyone ahead of him that is open for a layup. Secondly, when the steal is made and there is one or no defensive player contesting the ball, the ball handler dribbles the ball to the basket from either sideline area to get the layup or easy pass. Thirdly, when there are two or more players back defensively, the ball handler brings the ball down the middle of the floor for better passing angles unless the ball is stolen near his own basket in back court. When this happens, he should try to score immediately.

When the stealer takes the ball down the sideline, the fast breaking team wants two spots immediately filled. These spots are numbers 2 and 3 shown in *Diagram 7–53* with the dribbler coming down the right sideline from a steal. The first man possible should get to the spot where 2 is located, the low post area opposite the ball. The next man down the floor should fill the middle lane area where 3 is located. The back two men, where 4 and 5 are located should be the safeties. Their jobs are to stay behind the ball in case the defense steals it. These spots to fill when the ball is taken down the sideline are on a first come, first served basis.

When the dribbler takes the ball down the middle of the floor this usually means there are two or more defensive men back

Therefore, there are important spots for the other players to get to. Again, it is first come, first served. These spots are illustrated in *Diagram 7–54*. The 2 and 3 spots, outside lanes, should be filled first. The first ones in these spots take them and should call them vocally. The third spot to be taken is where 4 is located, the low post area. The last man becomes the safety man where 5 is shown. 1 always looks to score or to pass to the outside lanes or down low

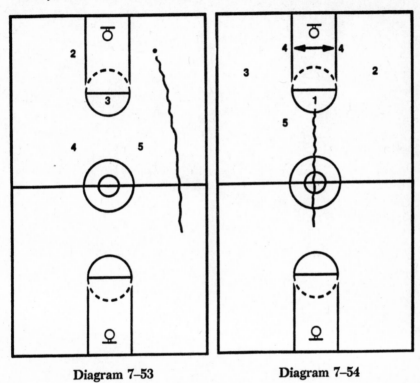

Diagram 7–53   Diagram 7–54

for a scoring opportunity. Players always look to take the 12 to 15 feet jumper and to take the ball inside.

    With these rules, the fast break will be effective. Many times the easy layup will come from the steal, but many times it will not. That is why rules exist for the fast break after a steal from the man to man press. It gives the break organization and achieves success.

Fans love to see the fast break following a steal from any type press. There is nothing more exciting to a fan than to see his team steal the ball from the opponent, create a fast break situation and score two points. This excitement is one of many reasons teams that utilize these types of fast breaking situations pack the gym night after night.

8

UTILIZING CONDITIONING
PROGRAMS FOR FAST
BREAK BASKETBALL

A top flight conditioning program is a necessity for developing a good fast break. A team cannot expect to run successfully if it is not in the proper condition. Basketball is a strenuous sport and sometimes athletes overlook the importance of year-round conditioning in keeping up endurance and stamina. Many teams with good, quick talent have been unable to win the big games because their players ran out of gas in the last quarter. Nothing is more disheartening than to see a good fast breaking team fold at the end of a game because of not being in shape.

The conditioning program can be divided into three phases:

pre-season, in season, and post season. Players will be in condition year round when this program is followed. We ask the players to commit themselves to the total program. They must do a lot of things on their own in the off-season. If a player is dedicated to doing these things, whether his coach is supervising him or not, he is a quality athlete. If not, a coach does not want him around in the long run, anyway. He is usually the type that will let the team down in clutch situations.

John Wooden once said that for teams to be successful the players must "execute the fundamentals, play team ball, and *be in top condition*." This is true beyond any doubt.

PRE-SEASON

Pre-season programs should last from three to four weeks and should stress quickness, agility, and endurance. These are characteristics that are necessary in the development of a good basketball team.

The following three week program is a program that can be used on a daily basis from the first through the third week and takes the team right into the in-season program.

First Week

Monday	*Stretching exercises*
	Ropejumping
	a. 100 forward
	b. 100 reverse
	c. 100 cross over
	Rim touching
	a. 25 right hand
	b. 25 left hand
	c. 25 both hands
	Backward Running
	a. One 25 yard dash
	b. One 50 yard dash

Lateral Running
(to be executed like the defensive slide)
20 yards, 3 sets
One 50 yard sprint (timed)
One mile run
One 50 yard dash (timed)

Tuesday
Stretching exercises

Rope jumping
  (same as Monday)
Rim touching
  (same as Monday)

Backward Running

a. One 30 yard dash
b. One 55 yard dash

Lateral Running

20 yards, 4 sets
Three 50 yard sprints
One mile run
Two 100 yard dashes (timed)

Wednesday
Stretching Exercises

Rope jumping (same)
Rim touching (same)
One mile run (timed)
One half mile fast walk
Four 50 yard sprints

Lateral Running

20 yards, 5 sets

Backward Running

a. One 35 yard
b. One 60 yard
One 100 yard dash
One mile run

Thursday
Stretching exercises

Rope jumping (same)
Rim touching (same)
Five 50 yard sprints

Three 100 yard dashes
One 440 yard dash

Lateral Running

20 yards, 6 sets

Backward Running

a. One 40 yard dash
b. One 65 yard dash
One mile run
One half mile fast walk
Five 50 yard dashes

Friday   *Stretching exercises*

Rope jumping (same)
Rim touching (same)
One half mile job
2 mile run (timed)

Lateral running

20 yards, 6 sets

Backward running

Two 50 yard dashes
Two 440 yard dashes
Three 50 yard dashes

Second Week

Monday   *Stretching exercises*

Rope jumping
a. 150 forward
b. 150 reverse
c. 150 cross over
Rim touching
a. 35 right hand
b. 35 left hand
c. 35 both hands
One mile run (timed)

Lateral running

20 yards, 6 sets

Backward running
a. One 45 yard dash
b. One 70 yard dash
One mile run
One 440 yard dash
Five 50 yard sprints

Tuesday

Stretching exercises
Rope jumping (same as Monday, Second Week)
Rim touching (same as Monday, Second Week)

Four 100 yard dashes
One 660 yard run

Lateral running
a. 20 yards, 7 sets

Backward running
a. One 50 yard dash
b. One 75 yard dash
Two mile run
One half fast walk
Five 50 yard sprints

Wednesday

Stretching exercises
Rope jumping (same)
Rim touching (same)
Four 100 yard dashes
One 660 yard run

Lateral running
20 yards, 8 sets

Backward running
a. One 55 yard dash
b. One 80 yard dash
One mile run
Five 50 yard sprints
One mile run

Thursday

Stretching exercises
Rope jumping (same)
Rim touching (same)

Backward running

a. One 60 yard dash
b. One 85 yard dash

Lateral Running

20 yards, 9 sets
One 660 yard run
Five 100 yard dashes
One mile jog
Five 50 yard sprints
One 660 yard run

Friday   *Stretching exercises*

Rope jumping (same)
Rim touching (same)
Three mile run (timed)

Backward running

Three 50 yard dashes

Lateral Running

20 yards, 10 sets
One mile jog

Third Week

Monday   *Stretching exercises*

Rope jumping
a. 175 forward
b. 175 reverse
c. 175 cross over
Rim touching
a. 40 right hand
b. 40 left hand
c. 40 both hands
One mile run (timed)

Lateral running

20 yards, 11 sets

Backward running

a. One 65 yard dash

b. One 90 yard dash
One 660 yard run
Three 100 yard dashes
One mile run
Three 50 yard sprints
One mile jog

Tuesday	*Stretching exercises*

Rope jumping (same as Monday, Third Week)
Rim touching (same as Monday, Third Week)

Lateral running

20 yards, 12 sets

Backward running

a. One 70 yard dash
b. One 95 yard dash
One 880 yard run
Four 50 yard sprints
One mile run
Four 100 yard dashes
One mile jog

Wednesday	*Stretching exercises*

Rope jumping (same)
Rim touching (same)
One mile run (timed)

Lateral running

20 yards, 7 sets
Five 100 yard dashes
Five 50 yard sprints

Backward running

One 75 yard dash
One mile run
One 100 yard dash
One mile run

Thursday	*Stretching exercises*

Rope jumping (same)
Rim touching (same)

Three mile run

Lateral running

20 yards, 7 sets
One mile jog
20 yards, 7 sets

Backward running

One 100 yard dash
One 880 yard run
One 100 yard dash
Four 100 yard dashes
Five 50 yard sprints

Friday   *Stretching exercises*

Rope jumping
a. 200 forward
b. 200 reverse
c. 100 cross over
Rim touching
a. 50 right hand
b. 50 left hand
c. 50 both hands
One 100 yard dash
Four mile run

Lateral running

20 yards, 15 sets

Backward running

Two 100 yard dashes
One 440 yard run
Five 50 yard dashes

It is important to allow the players to rest between sprints or runs. This is needed to get the maximum results from the players. A good procedure to follow is rest 1 minute after a short run (100 yards or less) and 3 minutes for anything run longer. This helps to avoid injury. *Do not run this program without proper resting periods between exercises.*

IN SEASON

This phase of the program follows the pre-season program and starts at the beginning of practice and lasts until the last game of the season.

In-season conditioning consists of going through all drills and techniques of basketball practice at 100% speed and effort; post practice running; eating and sleeping properly; avoiding unnecessary sicknesses or ailments; and running the mile run under a certain time limit. The health habits are important year round, but we supervise this aspect to the hilt during the season. The players must eat three meals a day, eating plenty of meat, fruit, and vegetables, while avoiding greasy foods as much as possible. Players should not eat between meals. Adequate sleep with regular hours is important. Each player should get at least eight hours of sleep each night. On the night before a game everybody's lights are out at 11:00 p.m.

The following suggestions can help eliminate common physical ailments and minor injuries and must be emphasized to the players on the first day of practice: consult the trainer, coach, or parents at the first sign of a cold; treat athletes foot, jock itch, cuts, or bruises immediately after practice; shower after every practice or game, but do not go outside without drying off; weigh in every day and if there is an unusual amount of weight lost consult the trainer.

The in-season program includes a timed mile run. On the first day of practice everybody will run the mile. All players 6' 6" and above must run the mile in 5 minutes and 45 seconds. All players below 6' 6" must run the mile in 5 minutes and 30 seconds. Nobody should be allowed to participate in team practice until he runs the mile in his specified time. Players are timed only once a day. Some players may miss a week of practice trying to get their times down. This is unnecessary and can be eliminated if the player will condition himself properly during the off season. If he misses practice on account of the mile run, he is only hurting himself because the other players are on the floor getting prepared while he is not.

Practices from the first day until the week of the first game last approximately two hours and fifteen minutes. During the season until February, practices should last approximately one hour and thirty minutes. On February 1, practices can be cut to approximately one hour. On days before a game practice will probably last no less than thirty minutes and no longer than an hour. These procedures for conditioning will enable the players to give 100% of their effort physically and mentally during the season. At the end of each practice, except the day before a game, we do post practice running. Our post practice running consists of lane sprinting, suicide sprints, or the army sliding drill.

Lane sprinting is simply sprints from one end of the basketball floor to the other. Suicide sprints, *Diagram 8–1*, consist of starting at the end line in back court and sprinting to the free-throw line extended area in back court and back to the end line in back court; to the half court line and back to the end line in back court; to the free-throw line extended area in front court back to the end line in back court. The last leg is the sprint full court and back.

The Army sliding drill, *Diagram 8–2*, is a conditioning drill adapted from one used by Bobby Knight, head basketball coach at Indiana University, when he was at Army. The drill has the player start at the end line in back court, sprint to half court, run backwards to the free-throw line, laterally slide to the right sideline and at this point do 10 fingertip pushups, laterally slide to the left sideline and do 10 fingertip pushups, sprint to the backboard in the front court and touch the rim 25 times while continuously jumping, laterally slide to the right sideline, and sprint the length of the floor.

This in-season conditioning program is conducive to winning. By following it the players will take the floor in any game at anytime of the season in top flight condition to give 100% effort.

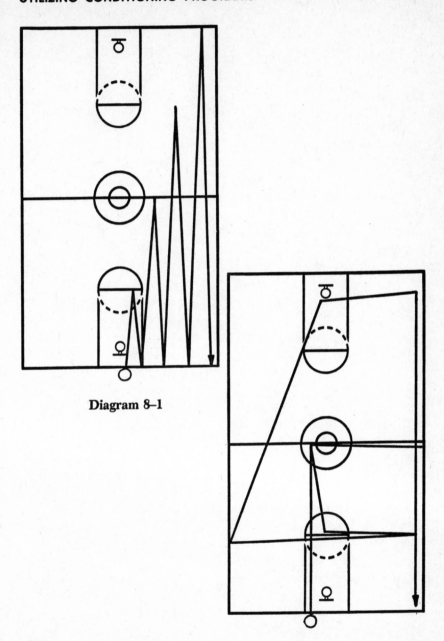

Diagram 8–1

Diagram 8–2

POST SEASON

The post season program should consist of a five to six week weight lifting program after the playing season, running, and playing.

It is a known fact that weight lifting will increase muscular strength and endurance. Weights, for example, will improve a player's vertical jump, an important characteristic in a basketball player. Rebounding, which is a major aspect of basketball, is sometimes determined by the amount of spring a player has in his legs. Time should be spent strengthening the quadriceps and calf muscles so that the player can increase his jumping ability.

Time should be spent developing the muscles that are weakest. Unnecessary time can be spent in the weight room trying to develop or add more strength to the legs of a player who has good spring and strength in his legs. Usually, if a player has good leg strength, he is apt to be weaker in the arms, shoulders, and hands. More time should be spent on these muscles instead of the legs. This does not mean to omit the legs altogether, but to concentrate more on the upper portion of the body.

In all weight exercise each player should have a partner to prevent accidents and to help arrange weights on shoulders when necessary. It is important that proper weight lifting techniques be used to avoid ruptures and strains.

The post season program should be supervised. A player will put forth more effort when someone is with him. Players like to show someone how much they can press and get satisfaction out of doing so.

The weight program should provide incentive. Charts should be posted in the weight room and include statistics, such as weight lifted, most overall strength added, most overall added inches to the body, and increased vertical jump. On the first day of weight lifting the vertical jump of each player should be measured. This can be found by measuring his fully extended reach while standing flat footed against a wall. Then the individual should jump as high as possible from a closed crouch position. The difference in inches between the jump measurement and standing position measurement is the player's vertical jumping power. At the conclusion of the program the trainer can utilize this same test to note the improvement.

Each player should have a goal in the off season weight program. If he needs to increase his vertical jump he must set his sights on increasing his leg strength. If he needs more arm or shoulder strength, his goal might be to press three fourths his weight by the end of the weight program.

Enthusiasm on the part of the coaching staff is a must for a successful weight program. If coaches are not enthusiastic then the players will not be. This enthusiasm in the off season can instill pride, a necessary ingredient to winning consistently. Pride cannot be instilled in a player at game time. Pride comes from a total commitment year round by the coaches and players to do their best during the season and in the off season as well.

A sufficient weight program is done three times a week, Monday, Wednesday, and Friday. The program should consist of the following exercises:

1. *Clean and Press*—Barbell is lifted from the floor to the front of the chest, and then pressed vertically to arm's length. The usual beginning weight is in accordance to the strength of the player. The usual procedure is to use weights with which the player can do this exercise 10 repetitions.

2. *Curl*—Barbell is held in hands with palms facing outward in front of thighs. From a standing position curl bar to chest and return to the starting position. Repeat the number of desired times. Beginning weight is normally around 50 pounds.

3. *Press*—Barbell is held at chest level and extended upward until the arms are straight above the individual. Players should use a weight that permits him to do this exercise 10 times.

4. *Toe Raises*—Using as much weight as possible, start at a standing position with the bar on the shoulders. Raise up on the toes and return to the starting position. The player should do this as many times as possible.

5. *Bent over Rowing*—The player keeps the legs straight, back straight, and bends the body at the waist. The bar should be hanging at arm's length. Pull the bar up until it touches the middle of the chest, then lower. Use enough weight to do 10 repetitions.

6. *Three Quarter Squat*—From a standing position with the barbell on shoulders, the player lowers the body into a three quarter squat position and then returns to the starting position. Using weights half the individual's body weight, he repeats the exercise 10 times.

7. *Situps*—From a prone position with the hands clasped behind the head, the player comes to a full sitting position touching elbow to opposite knee. He does this exercise as many times as possible.

8. *Three Quarter Knee Bend and Press Behind the Neck*—With the barbells on the shoulders, the player lowers the body to a three quarter squat position and, as he rises, pushes the barbell upward until the arms are straight above him, then lowers the weight to the back of the neck. He repeats 10 times using half his own body weight.

The program usually consists of one set but you can utilize any number of sets you feel is sufficient for your team. It is very important that the players loosen up before lifting the weights. This is done to avoid injuries.

Weight training programs have proven to be successful to basketball programs. The game itself is not designed to develop strength, yet requires strength for success. Many potentially great basketball players are not successful because they are too weak. Weight training can help overcome this deficiency and enable a potentially good basketball player who lacks strength to become stronger and greatly enhance his chances of being successful on the basketball floor. Many skinny basketball players have developed their bodies through weight training.

After the weight lifting on Monday, Wednesday, and Friday, the players should run a timed mile to keep up their endurance and stamina.

Players can be allowed to play on their own in the post season.

They should play full court with members of the team as often as possible to keep in condition and get the feel of each other's play. Players can learn about each other's game in the off season by studying moves, shots, and other phases of the game that sometimes go unrecognized during the regular season.

The post season program is an integral part of a basketball program. Without it, other teams can get ahead of you. Through the use of a post season program players will maintain their condition, increase their strength, and have the confidence and pride that it takes to win basketball games.

9

DRILLS TO PERFECT
THE FAST BREAK

The success of the fast break depends upon the type of players a team has and the amount of time spent in practice to develop the fast break. Fast breaking requires quickness, fundamentals, timing, team play, conditioning, and aggressiveness on the part of each player. To develop a good fast break a team must perfect these qualities through the use of drills in daily practice sessions. Drills are a must in teaching the fast break.

There are many drills to use in perfecting the fast break, including rebounding drills, outlet pass drills, two lane drills, three lane drills, and four man drills. These drills can be used in the early part of the season and during the playing season to improve the qualities that are necessary to the success of the fast break.

Each player performs in each of these drills because at some time during the season each player will be involved in fast break situations.

Just as learning multiplication tables starts at 1, the fast break should be taught with drills from the beginning level (the rebound) and worked until the product is refined at the finish. The fast break drills allow a team to perfect the fast break in all its phases.

REBOUNDING DRILLS

The initial phase of the fast break is the defensive rebound. If players are not consistently successful in getting this, they cannot expect to be a good fast breaking team and can count on losing. Therefore, blocking out is a must. These rebounding drills consist of the "rip-off" rebound, one on one block out, two on two block out, three on three block out, and the shooter block out.

Each player should rebound the ball like a wild animal. This is called the rip-off rebound and is pictured in *Diagram 9–1*. When the manager shoots the ball off the backboard (not the rim) on the player's side, the player leaps as high as possible with arms extended to get the ball quickly. When he gets the ball he is to growl like a lion. As he grasps the ball, the player should literally rip the ball off the boards keeping the elbows spread, come down with the ball in his hands, and form a wide base with the feet well apart.

A basic one on one blocking out drill is illustrated in *Diagram 9–2*. The manager can line up to shoot the ball from any area of the floor within fifteen feet of the basket. When the manager shoots, X, the defensive man, will face the basket and block the defender from the basket with his body. He must feel the offensive man with his buttocks and hands to keep the offensive player from getting in front of him. When the ball comes off the board, the defender must execute the "rip-off" rebound.

The two on two block out drill, *Diagram 9–3*, uses the same techniques as described in the one on one block out drill, but congests the lane area more by adding another couple. The offensive men, O, line up at the corners of the free-throw line. The defensive men, X, play between their men and the basket.

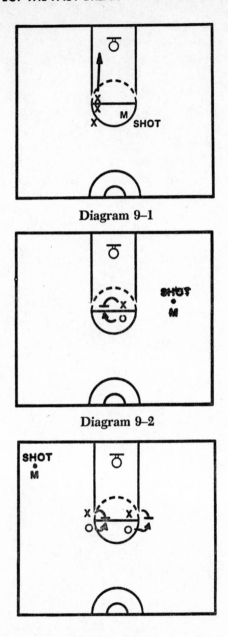

Diagram 9–1

Diagram 9–2

Diagram 9–3

The three on three block out drill is illustrated in *Diagram 9–4*. In this drill, a cup is formed around the basket. The players use the same blocking out techniques as described in the one on one block out drill.

The shooter block out drill, *Diagram 9–5*, emphasizes not letting the shooter get his own rebound. Shooters are told to follow their shots and if they are not blocked out they have a good chance of getting the offensive rebound. The defensive man X, pressures the shooter, O. When the shot is taken O will go for the offensive rebound. X is to block the shooter out and then go get the rebound.

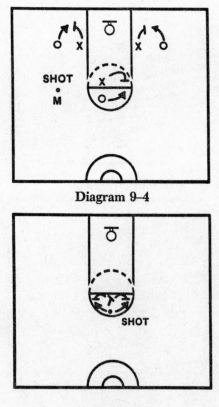

Diagram 9–4

Diagram 9–5

OUTLET PASS DRILLS

Once the ball has been rebounded the outlet pass is usually made to get the fast break working. The outlet pass is a crucial part of the fast break and there are a variety of drills to help perfect the outlet pass.

A drill called the jumping outlet is shown in *Diagram 9–6.* The manager shoots the ball from the free-throw line and shoots to miss. The rebounder is to retrieve the ball while he is in mid-air, turn and fire the outlet pass to any of the three outlet men before his feet touch the floor. This drill emphasizes a quick outlet and stresses accuracy with the pass.

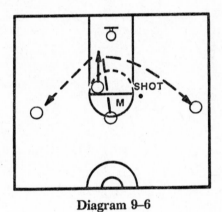

Diagram 9–6

Diagram 9–7 illustrates the length-of-the-floor outlet drill to use to improve the accuracy of the length of the floor pass. The manager shoots to miss from the free-throw line. Rebounders start near the free-throw line in back court and the receivers start at the time line. When the shot is missed the rebounder gets the ball and makes one power dribble with a long stride, leaps into the air and throws the ball the length of the floor to the receiver who has left the time line at the rebound, heading for the basket for the layup. Many players are weak at throwing this pass and many have trouble catching it so it is very useful at developing the player in both these areas.

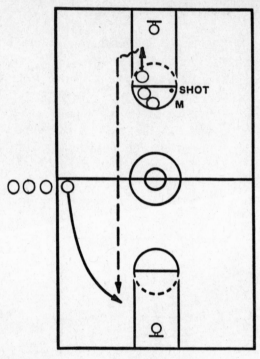

Diagram 9-7

The regular outlet pass drill we use is shown in *Diagrams 9-8* and *9-9*, which illustrate the technique on both sides of the floor. *Diagram 9-8* illustrates the rebounder, O, getting the ball and making the outlet pass on the right side of the floor to 02. X, the defender, is to try to deflect the outlet pass. This same situation is shown in *Diagram 9-9* on the left side of the floor.

This drill has another phase that is added after this drill has been perfected and is shown in *Diagram 9-10*. The drill remains the same except a defender, who is added to the receiver of the outlet pass, tries to keep the outlet pass from being completed. This makes the outlet passer develop more accuracy and makes the receiver work to get the ball.

A drill, called off-the-move outlet, is shown in *Diagram 9-11*. 1 is the rebounder who takes the missed shot and fires the outlet pass to 2 on the move from the baseline area to the middle of the floor. This drill makes the outlet passer be accurate to a target on the move.

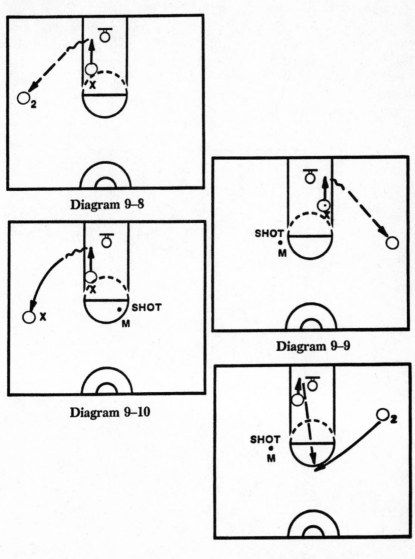

Diagram 9–8

Diagram 9–10

Diagram 9–9

Diagram 9–11

TWO MAN DRILLS

A two man fast break drill known as the two on none drill, *Diagram 9–12*, is a drill used by Sonny Allen of S.M.U. This drill develops passing and catching skills while moving fast. The players line up in two lines about 15 feet apart underneath the basket. The players in each line pass the ball between them the length of the floor and make the layup. They repeat this procedure while coming back down the court. This drill emphasizes passing and catching properly. The players are to keep the ball moving without making such mistakes as walking.

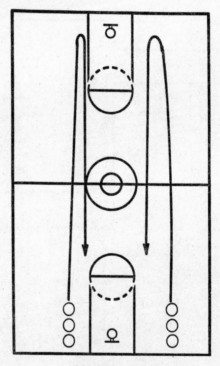

Diagram 9–12

The two on one fast break drill, *Diagram 9–13*, is a common fast break drill that can be used almost daily. Most coaches will probably use the full court for the two-on-one drill. The two offensive men, O, are near both sidelines staying wide in the outside lanes. The dribbler takes the ball to the basket and either shoots the layup or passes to his teammate for the layup. X, the defender, has the responsibility of keeping both men from shooting the layup.

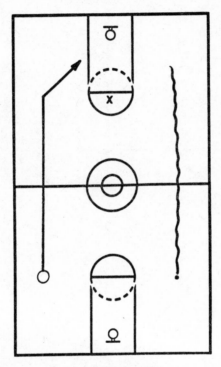

Diagram 9–13

The two on two drill, *Diagram 9–14*, is a drill to use to perfect the fast break when a situation exists that has the opponent with as many people back defensively as the offense has attacking. The offensive men 1 and 2, 1 with the ball, advance into the front court and try to score creating two men games, such as the pick "n" roll, if a layup does not occur. X, the defense, tries to prevent the score.

A two lane rebounding drill is illustrated in *Diagram 9–15*. 1, the rebounder, gets the missed shot the manager shoots, makes the outlet pass to 2 who fills the middle, and fills the outside lane to either side, left lane in this example. 1 passes to 2 for the layup as he makes his angle cut to the basket.

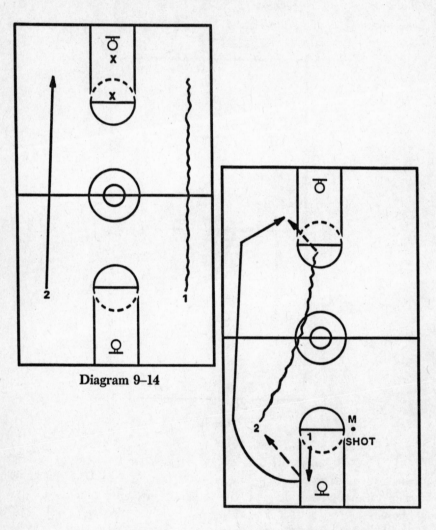

Diagram 9–14

Diagram 9–15

THREE MAN DRILLS

Three man fast break drills are the most popular fast break drills in the U.S.A. This is due to the importance of filling the three lanes properly.

The three on none drill, *Diagram 9–16*, is another drill developed by Sonny Allen. It develops proper dribbling and passing skills for the man in the middle lane, 1. It also develops proper running techniques for the men in the outside lanes, 2 and 3. The 1 man starts at the free-throw line in the back court. 2 and 3 are wide just inside the sidelines. When 1 puts the ball on the floor the threesome advances down the floor. 1 dribbles to the free-throw line area in front court and passes to 2 or 3 for the layup.

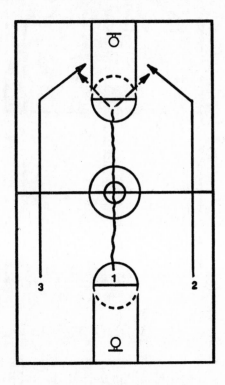

Diagram 9–16

The three on one drill is then added, *Diagram 9–17*, and the offensive men perform the same techniques. A defensive man, X, is at the free-throw line area in front court and tries to stop the score. The dribbler, 1, must make the defensive man commit so that he can pass off to 2 or 3. This drill can be set up to bring these same players back by placing a defensive man on both ends of the floor. Upon scoring, the offensive men return to the other end of the floor.

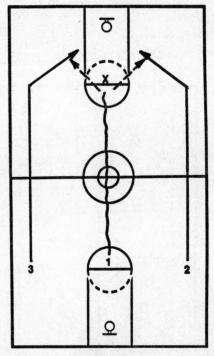

Diagram 9–17

Diagram 9–18 shows the setup of a very useful drill, the three on two fast break drill. The drill is done in groups of threes. The defense, X1 through X6, are on both ends of the court. The drill is started by 1 dribbling the ball up the floor with 2 and 3 in the outside lanes, *Diagram 9–19*. These three men try to score on the

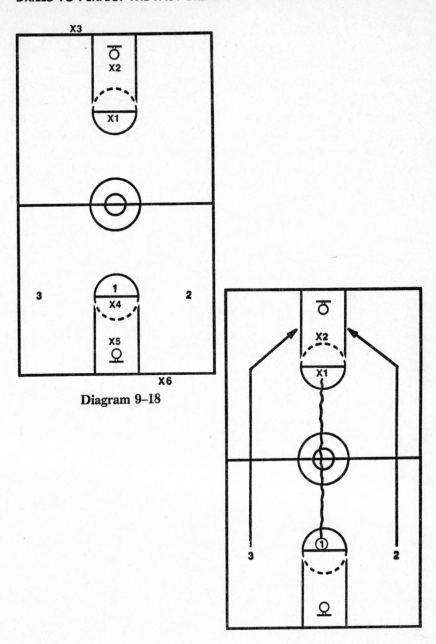

Diagram 9–18

Diagram 9–19

defense X1 and X2 initially. X3 is allowed to come in and play defense on a shot or the second pass by the offense. This means that the offense must take advantage of the three on two situation quickly or there will not be any advantage. If the offense scores or the defense gets the rebound, X1 and X2, and X3 fill the three lanes and fast break back down the floor in the same manner as 1, 2, and 3. There are no certain lanes for X1, X2, and X3 to fill.

Diagram 9–20 is an example of the defense rebounding the ball and fast breaking back to the other end of the floor. The drill continues until the coach ends it. It is a great conditioning drill in addition to helping develop passing, dribbling, lane filling, and shooting from the fast break.

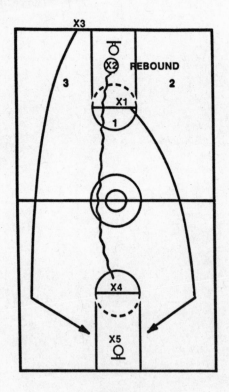

Diagram 9–20

The three on three drill, *Diagram 9–21*, is run the same as the three on two drill except that the third defensive man is allowed in the front court to pick up an offensive man. If the men in the three lanes, 1, 2, or 3 do not score a layup, they play a three man game offensively trying to score against the defense. If the offense scores or the defense gets the rebound, they return the fast break to the defense at the other end of the floor.

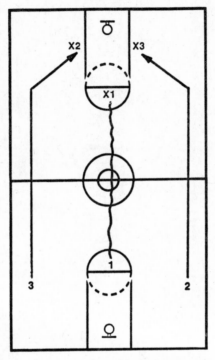

Diagram 9–21

A drill called the three man outlet is shown in *Diagram 9–22*. 1 is the rebounder and 2 and 3 are the outlet receivers. 1 rebounds the ball and makes the outlet pass to 3. 2 cuts to the middle and receives the pass from 3. 2 fills the middle lane with the ball and 3

the left outside lane. The rebounder, 1, always fills the outside lane
away from the outlet pass, in this case the right outside lane. The
three offensive men attack the defensive man, X, at the opposite
end of the floor. This drill is very effective in teaching the rebounder to quickly fill a lane after rebounding.

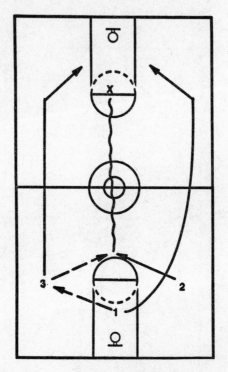

Diagram 9–22

Another three lane outlet is illustrated in *Diagram 9–23*. 1
rebounds and outlets the ball to 3 who fills the middle lane. 1 goes
opposite the outlet pass at all times and in this situation fills the left
outside lane. 2 fills the right outside lane. The three offensive men,
1, 2, and 3 attack the two defensive men X. When the offense loses

possession, they will sprint back staying off the playing floor and the next three offensive men will attack the defense.

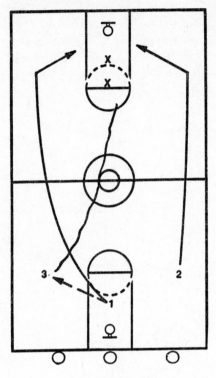

Diagram 9–23

The three man figure eight drill is shown in *Diagram 9–24*. This drill improves passing and catching skills for a more effective fast break. No dribbling is allowed. The rule of thumb for the offensive man is to always go behind the man he passes the ball to. The drill starts with 1 passing the ball to 2 and continues until a layup is made on the other end of the floor at which time three more players will run the drill.

The drill known as the three man score drill, *Diagram 9–25*, is used to help perfect the fast break after an opponent has scored.

The ball is shot by a manager or coach in the free-throw line area. 1 takes it out of the net, in-bounds it quickly to 2, and fills the right outside lane. 2 fills the middle lane with the ball and 3 is responsible for the left outside lane. In this drill the coach should stress getting a shot within 4 and one half seconds after the ball comes through the net. Also, there should be no more than 3 dribbles between the two key areas by 2. Defense can be added to this drill at the opposite end of the floor at the coach's discretion.

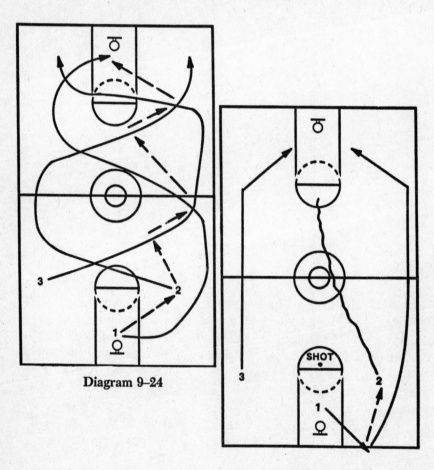

Diagram 9–24

Diagram 9–25

A three versus four drill to use in developing the fast break is shown in *Diagram 9–26*. 1 is the rebounder and can make the outlet pass to either 2 or 3 and fills the lane opposite his pass. The outlet receiver fills the middle lane with the ball and the other outlet fills the outside lane on his side. Defensive man X1 is responsible for trying to steal the outlet pass to either side. X2 pressures the dribbler in the middle lane looking to create a turnover. X3 and X4 play defense in the front court should the fast break get past X1 or X2.

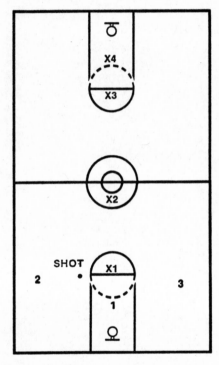

Diagram 9–26

This drill can be advanced to a three versus five drill, *Diagram 9–27*, by adding a defensive man, X5, to try to keep 1 from rebounding the missed shot, and if 1 does rebound the ball, X5 forces him to make a bad outlet pass. The offense 1, 2, and 3 have the objectives of overcoming all the defensive obstacles and scoring at their end of the floor.

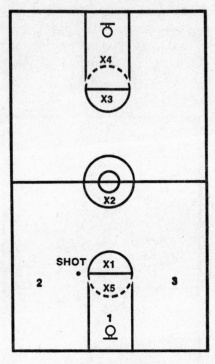

Diagram 9–27

FOUR MAN DRILLS

Four man drills are the final buildup to the five man fast break. The four man drills start with a four on none drill then build up to four on one, four on two, four on three, and four on four drills.

The four on none drill is shown in *Diagram 9–28*. The manager shoots the ball from the free-throw line area. 3 and 4 are the rebounders. The one that rebounds the ball is a trailer and the other will fill the outside lane away from the outlet pass. 1 and 2 are the outlet receivers. The outlet receiver on the side of the rebound breaks to the sideline outlet area and the other receiver breaks to the middle. In *Diagram 9–28*, 3 rebounds the ball and makes the outlet pass to 1. 1 passes to 2 and fills the left outside lane. 2 fills the middle lane with the ball. 4, the offside rebounder, fills the right outside lane. 3, the rebounder, fills the trailer lane staying behind the ball until the ball is passed to a wing. When this happens, he will go to the low post on the side of the ball. If 1, 2, or 3 shoots the layup, he stays behind the ball. Layups, jump shots, and passes to the low post can be worked on in this drill.

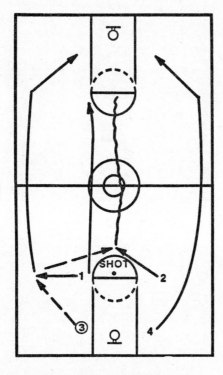

Diagram 9–28

The four on one drill, *Diagram 9–29*, utilizes the same offensive techniques, but adds a defensive man in the front court. The defensive man is to try and stop the score. In this illustration the drill is run with 4 rebounding the ball. 2 receives the outlet, passes to 1 in the middle lane, and fills the right outside lane. 3 fills the left outside lane opposite the outlet pass. 4, the rebounder is the trailer.

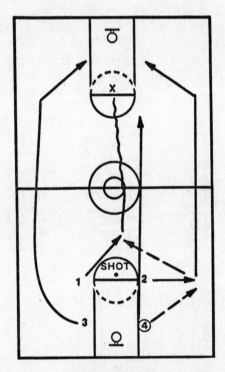

Diagram 9–29

The next phase of the four man drills is the four on two drill, *Diagram 9–30*. In this drill there are two defensive men in the front court to stop the four man fast break.

Three men attack defensively in the four on three drill, *Diagram 9–31*. In this situation, the trailer will start receiving a lot of

passes down low from the wing. The three lanes have been filled by
1, 2, and 3. 4 is the trailer. In this example 1 has passed to 3 in the
left outside lane. 4 in the trailer lane posts up low on the ball side
and receives the pass for a score from 3.

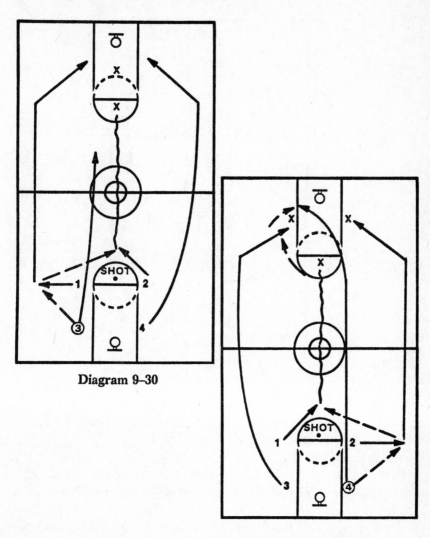

Diagram 9–30

Diagram 9–31

The four on four drill is illustrated in *Diagram 9–32* with 3 rebounding the ball. The offensive techniques remain the same as the four on three except that there are four defensive men on the front court.

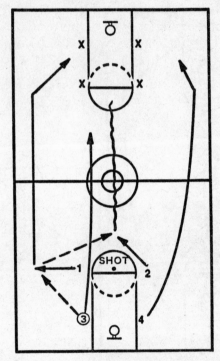

Diagram 9–32

Another drill, called the 4 on 3 plus 1 drill, is shown in *Diagram 9–33*. Offensive techniques remain the same as the four on none drill. In this drill there is a defensive man at mid-court, X1. His job is to try to create a turnover in this area. Three other defensive men, X2, X3, and X4 try to stop the score if the ball is penetrated into the front court.

It is sometimes advantageous to work the four man drills against five defensive men in the front court, pictured in *Diagram*

9–34. This is usually done around mid-season and makes the offensive fast break work harder to get the shot.

Without the drills discussed here the fast break will probably not be successful. A team cannot run all these drills in one day, but over a season's period these drills can help a team have a more effective fast break. Changing up these drills daily also takes the boredom out of running only the same drills each day. Players enjoy a variety of drills, and it helps them become more effective when running the fast break in a game.

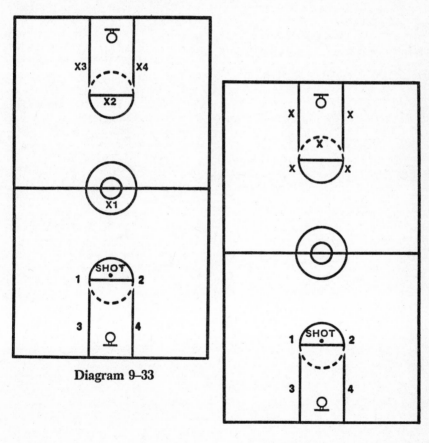

Diagram 9–33

Diagram 9–34

INDEX

Made field goal *(cont.)*
post play rules, 77-78
right outside lane, 75
second guard, 75
set break, 78
small forward, 75
man to man full court pressure, 81-84
"pin" technique, 82
V cut technique, 82
post man technique, 72-74
baseball pass, 73
brings ball in-bounds, 72
not stand under goal, 72
not use square stance, 73
quickness, 74
running an entire game, 71
Made free-throw, 101-109
Man to man full court pressure, 81-84
Man to man press, 163-166
Meals, 175
Middle lane, 30, 31
Middle pass, 87
Missed field goal:
controlled break, 62-70
sideline break, 57-62
two guard break, 42-57
Missed free-throw, 94-101

N

Newton, C.M., 106

O

Odds, 29-30
Off-season conditioning, 168
Off-the-move outlet, 188, 189
One on one block out drill, 184, 185
1-3-1 trap, 154-163
1-3-1 zone:
controlled break, 63, 67, 133
corner area and out front, 131
coverages, 128-129
lane filling, 131
movement of men, 131
passing of ball, 131
penetration, 131
sideline break, 133
slides, 128-129, 130, 131
strengths, 131
two guard break, 55, 56, 131
wing areas, 131
1-2-1-1 full court zone press, 85
1-2-1-1 zone press, 136-146

1-2-2 zone:
ball at left wing area, 121, 122
ball at right wing area, 121, 122
ball in left corner, 123
ball is out front, 121, 122
controlled break, 63, 67, 126-127
defensing the perimeter, 121
outside lanes break way to corners, 124
penetration of ball, 121
right corner slides, 123
sideline break, 127
spread type, 121
two guard break, 55, 56, 124-125
vulnerable, 121
weaknesses in lane area, 121
X maneuver, 126
Organization, 19
Outlet man, 28
Outlet pass drills:
jumping, 187
length-of-floor, 187
off-the-move, 188, 189
regular, 188
Outlet passes, 25, 28, 31
Outside lanes, 30, 31
Overhead pass, 25

P

Passes:
back, 25
baseball, 25
bounce, 25, 28
chest, 25, 28
left hand for support, 25
outlet, 25, 28
overhead, 25
right handed baseball, 25
Pressing defenses:
man to man press, 163-166
1-3-1 trap, 154-163
1-2-1-1 zone press, 136-146
2-2-1 zone press, 146-154
Personnel, two guard break, 56
Physical ailments, 175
Picks and maneuvers, 78
"Pin" technique, 82
Players, 19
Pop down technique, 64, 65
Post man, controlled break, 63
Post man technique, 72-74
Post season conditioning, 178-181
Post-up maneuver, 109-111
Practices, 176